BRITISH
BARROWS

BRITISH BARROWS

A MATTER OF LIFE AND DEATH

ANN WOODWARD

TEMPUS

Cover photograph by Francesca Radcliffe

First published 2000
Paperback edition first published 2002

PUBLISHED IN THE UNITED KINGDOM BY:
Tempus Publishing Ltd
The Mill, Brimscombe Port
Stroud, Gloucestershire GL5 2QG

PUBLISHED IN THE UNITED STATES OF AMERICA BY:
Tempus Publishing Inc.
2 Cumberland Street
Charleston, SC 29401

British Library Cataloguing in Publication Data.
A catalogue record for this book is available from the British Library.

ISBN 0 7524 1468 2

Typesetting and origination by Tempus Publishing.
PRINTED AND BOUND IN GREAT BRITAIN.

Contents

List of illustrations

Text figures

Colour plates

Preface

Barrows are collectively the most numerous and enduring monuments surviving from prehistoric Britain, and there exists a massive store of barrow data, much of which has never been synthesised or interpreted. This book uses a small sample of the available information in order to illustrate and develop some new approaches to their study. The pictures have been chosen to describe surviving monuments and their landscapes rather than to illustrate their excavation. The results of excavation are covered primarily by written descriptions of certain key sequences, while aspects of grave goods are presented in some simple tables and in photographs. Inevitably, in condensing the key sequences I have sometimes introduced new interpretations, and also a few errors of detail may have occurred; for these I alone am responsible. I have attempted to cover as many regions of Britain as possible, and to concentrate on areas and sites which are a little less well known (**1**). As I happen to live in Dorset there is a noticeable bias to sites in that county, but this is also deliberate in that I have attempted to avoid the usual dependence on the better known barrows of Wiltshire. There will be a few detailed studies of the very well preserved barrow cemeteries around Stonehenge, but I hope that such aspects will be balanced by in-depth consideration of ploughed-out barrows, especially in Yorkshire and on the river gravels of middle England.

My interest in barrows is long lived and has been stimulated by many archaeologists. In recent years I have benefited particularly from discussions with David Field, Gwilym Hughes and my husband, Peter Woodward. Much of the Dorset fieldwork and research has been undertaken with Peter Woodward, and I am particularly grateful to him for support throughout, and for reading and commenting on the text. In the field we were often accompanied by our daughter Alice who has probably visited the Lanceborough King Barrow more times than any child since the Bronze Age. For many years of stimulation studying the barrows around Stonehenge I am grateful to Vince Gaffney, Ron Yorston and Sally Exon. Some of the results of our joint project in this area will be referred to in this book, and the full report will be published soon. The computing aspects of that project were partly funded by a grant from The Nuffield Trust, and the drawings which appear here as figures **56** and **69** were drawn by Harry Buglass of the Department of Ancient History and Archaeology, University of Birmingham. I am grateful to them, and also to the Birmingham University Field Archaeology Unit who allowed me time to prepare the captions and bibliographic references. Peter Kemmis Betty encouraged me to write the book, and had the inspired idea of using a large body of pictures from the National Monuments Record (the public archive of English Heritage) to illustrate it. I am particularly grateful to Robin Taylor of English Heritage who has guided the necessary arrangements with the NMR, and to his colleagues Katy Whitaker and Chris Chandler. Francesca Radcliffe kindly supplied a separate series of her aerial photographs relating to barrows in Dorset. For other illustrations

I am grateful to Gwilym Hughes, Philip Rahtz and the Dorset Natural History and Archaeological Society. Figures **11**, **12**, **19**, **34**, **35**, **44**, **45**, **50**, **70**, **72**, **74** and **75** were drawn by Peter Woodward. Finally I thank my friend Elizabeth James who allowed me to borrow her copy of Hoare's *Ancient Wiltshire* for a long period of time.

The following illustrations from the National Monuments Record are Crown copyright: figures **2**, **3**, **8-9**, **13-15**, **23**, **25-29**, **32**, **33**, **36**, **37**, **39-43**, **46-49**, **51-53**, **55**, **66**, **67**, **69**, **71**, **73**; **colour plates 1**, **3**, **12**, **15** and **17**. Line illustrations have been copied from the following Royal Commission volumes: figures **6**, **7** and **31** (joint Crown and Cornwall Archaeological Unit copyright) from Johnson and Rose 1994, figures 24, 25 and 30; figures **14**, **32** and **42** from Smith 1979, figures 49, 6(b) and 10; figures **25**, **27** and **51** from Stoertz 1997, figures 17, 14 and 10; figures **26**, **69** and **71** from RCHME 1952, pages 228, 43 and 41; figures **28** and **36** from RCHME 1990, Area Plans 3 and 2; figure **46** from RCHME 1970, page 460; figure **49** from RCHME 1975, page 114; figures **3**, **8**, **13** and **39** from the forthcoming English Heritage volume, *Archaeology of the Salisbury Plain Training Area*, these last in advance of publication, with the kind permission of David Field and English Heritage. **Colour plates 9**, **11**, **13**, **16**, **22**, **25** and **26** are copyright Francesca Radcliffe; figure **22** is copyright Gwilym Hughes and Birmingham University Field Archaeology Unit; **colour plate 6** is copyright G. Norrie and Birmingham University Field Archaeology Unit; figures **20**, **21**, **54**, **58**, **59**, **60**, **62** and **colour plates 2**, **5**, **7**, **8**, **10** and **29** are copyright the Dorset Natural History and Archaeological Society at the Dorset County Museum; figures **4** and **57** are copyright Philip Rahtz; figures **5** and **10** are copyright The Prehistoric Society; figures **56** and **68** and **colour plates 21**, **27** and **28** are copyright Sally Exon, Vince Gaffney, Ann Woodward and Ron Yorston; figure **30** is copyright Cornwall Archaeological Unit; figure **38** is copyright Keiller Collection (held by NMR); **colour plates 4**, **22** and **23** were taken by Peter Leach. The cover picture is taken from an air photograph by Francesca Radcliffe.

1 *Distribution of major sites mentioned in the text*

1 Camster Round, Caithness	15 Deeping St. Nicholas, Lincolnshire	29 Nutbane, Hampshire
2 Masterton, Fife	16 Barnack, Cambridgeshire	30 Snail Down, Wiltshire
3 Mount Stuart, Bute	17 Little Cressingham, Norfolk	31 Stonehenge, Wiltshire
4 Arran	18 Radwell, Bedfordshire	32 Rockbourne, Hampshire
5 Ryedale, North Yorkshire	19 Roxton, Bedfordshire	33 Oakley Down, Dorset
6 Loughcrew, Ireland	20 Black Mountains, South Wales	34 West Heath, West Sussex
7 Willerby Wold, Lincolnshire	21 Milton Keynes, Buckinghamshire	35 Knowlton, Dorset
8 Rudston, Yorkshire	22 Belas Knap, Gloucestershire	36 Simon's Ground, Dorset
9 Garton Slack, Yorkshire	23 Parc Le Broes Cwm, Gower	37 South Dorset
10 Pant-y-Saer, Anglesey	24 Devil's Quoits, Oxfordshire	38 Craddock Moor, Cornwall
11 Brenig, Denbighshire	25 Barrow Hills, Oxfordshire	39 Afton Down, Isle of Wight
12 Stanton Moor, Derbyshire	26 Wayland's Smithy, Oxfordshire	
13 Lockington, Leicestershire	27 Ashen Hill, Somerset	
14 Maxey, Cambridgeshire	28 Lambourn Seven Barrows, Berkshire	

1   The fascination of barrows

My formative years were spent in the shadow of the Berkshire Downs. As a child of the early 1950s, clouded by the Cold War, the Suez crisis, and official issue cod liver oil, outings to the Downs supplied welcome experiences of another world. This was a world of short springy turf, wild scabious and skylarks, and, on one of the walks, we visited The Wayland's Smithy. This is a stone chambered long barrow that was extensively excavated by Richard Atkinson and Stuart Piggott in 1962 and 1963. But when I visited it first the site was in its former ruinous state, a hidden and magical place. The stone chamber had been exposed and several of the capstones were fallen. One could crawl into the chambers, some of which were dark and cave-like (**2**), and contemplate the legend of the Wayland Smith. If you left your horse by the stones, along with a silver coin, the invisible smith, aided by his imp Flibbertigibbet, would shoe the horse. Following the excavation, the façade of huge sarsen stones was reconstructed, as shown in an archaeological record photograph taken by the Ordnance Survey (**colour plate 1**) The exciting, irregular configuration of the ruined chambers has gone, but the place, still surrounded by a circle of trees, retains its magical effect. Barrows were important and fascinating things, and many were built above or around the graves of people, and then were altered and enlarged over the years. They were monuments to the dead and home of the ancestors, but also mounds for the living. They marked out the land, defined pathways, acted as powerful symbols, and formed a major part of the perceived landscapes which welded nature and human history together in a seamless whole.

Barrows and archaeologists

The only reason that we know anything about barrows is because people of the present, and of the recent historic past, have been interested in them. People have looked at barrows, drawn and photographed them, described them in words, and dug into them to find out what might be inside. However, the growth in knowledge concerning prehistoric barrows has not been an even progression. Certain individuals have, through history, become fascinated by barrows and have pursued their investigations with ardent fervour. Thus the increase in knowledge has occurred in irregular jumps, with peaks and troughs of activity over the years. Many barrows were opened in the medieval period or earlier. Of these trenches and holes, and of the objects retrieved, there is little record. The same can be said for many of the excavations undertaken in the eighteenth and nineteenth centuries, but a series of antiquarian barrow diggers, working mainly in Yorkshire, Derbyshire, Wiltshire and Dorset, did describe and illustrate their results, and many weighty volumes were published. Some of these archaeologists recorded their work in more accurate detail than others, but the published descriptions, the surviving archives and the grave finds which have been preserved in local or national museum collections still provide one of the major sources for

2 *Wayland's Smithy, Oxfordshire, photographed by M. Wight in 1937.*
(© Crown copyright. NMR)

modern research on prehistoric barrows. The antiquarian tradition continued until the beginning of the twentieth century, by which time techniques of excavation had been heavily influenced by the work of General Pitt Rivers, who developed more systematic approaches to the preparation of measured site drawings, plots showing the find spots of selected objects, and scale illustrations of the finds — potsherds and fragments as well as the more complete and exotic items.

During the twentieth century, research into barrows followed three interrelated strands: ground survey, excavation and interpretation. Survey was advanced in two major ways, firstly by a single individual and secondly by a national institution. The individual was Leslie Grinsell, who between the 1930s and 1980s visited, measured and recorded every barrow in most of the southern English counties. Travelling by public transport and on foot he covered more ground, probably, than any other field archaeologist, spurred on by his fascination for barrows and the thought of a rewarding cream tea at the end of the day.

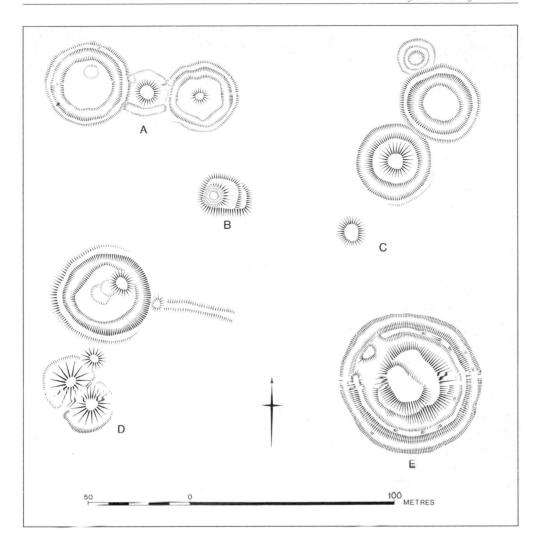

3 *Plans of selected round barrows on Salisbury Plain:*

A. *Silk Hill, two disc barrows with a smaller bell barrow placed in between.*

B. *Small bowl barrow with an external bank, close to the source of the Nine Mile River.*

C. *Silk Hill bowl barrow (top). The adjacent bank of the disc barrow straightens to avoid it, but marginally encroaches upon its ditch. The disc also impinges upon the massive bell barrow to its south. A bowl barrow lies a little further to the south.*

D. *Bulford Down, an irregular barrow resembling a disc, with a small bowl barrow overlapping the inner lip of the ditch. A smaller bowl barrow lies to the east immediately outside the ditch, adjacent to or perhaps on top of, a linear bank. To the south lie two confluent bowl barrows with a third bowl partly overlying the ditch of the northernmost.*

E. *Silk Hill, a large bell barrow with a two-phase mound and a bank placed around the inner lip of the ditch. Although the bank lies inside the ditch it is almost henge-like in appearance.*

(© Crown copyright. NMR)

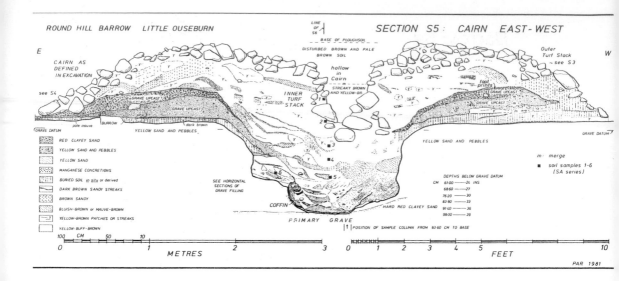

4 *Little Ouseburn, Yorkshire. Cross-section of the central Early Bronze Age grave and cairn, drawn by Philip Rahtz. Note the levels at which the coffin stain was drawn; the stains are shown in plan in figure* **57**

Other archaeologists who have spent large parts of their lives studying and recording archaeological sites on the ground are the field investigators of the Royal Commission on Historic Monuments (England), which is now part of English Heritage, and the Ordnance Survey. Working in a series of counties, and led by quiet and highly skilled workers like Collin Bowen and Isobel Smith, many barrows have been analysed and recorded in minute detail (**3**). Through such intricate analytical field survey it has often been possible to work out sequences of barrow construction through time, without resorting to the spade. Running concurrently with these developments there was also a substantial programme of modern barrow excavation. Much of this involved barrows which had been ploughed flat or were about to be destroyed (**colour plate 2**). Such work was instigated and funded by the Ministry of Public Building and Works, and was concentrated particularly in the period between 1950 and about 1970. The digging was carried out by a series of extremely talented excavators, including Charles Green, Faith Morgan (Vatcher), Philip Rahtz, Patricia Christie and, the most prolific of all, Paul Ashbee. From 1970 onwards there have been fewer barrows excavated on the chalk and limestone hills, but major campaigns of rescue excavation on the gravel terraces of rivers such as the Great Ouse, Welland, Trent and Thames were set in motion. Some of the results of these campaigns will be summarised in the pages of this book. The developments in both survey and excavation were linked to the refinement of techniques of archaeological drawing. In the days of hand illustration, individual styles of draughtsmanship became highly developed and were able to impart a unique and valuable contribution within the published reports on barrow excavations (**4**). And more stylised approaches could combine information concerning plans, cross section, buried details and grave goods, in innovative and interesting ways (**5**). On the other hand, the ongoing work of the Royal Commission encouraged the development of intricate

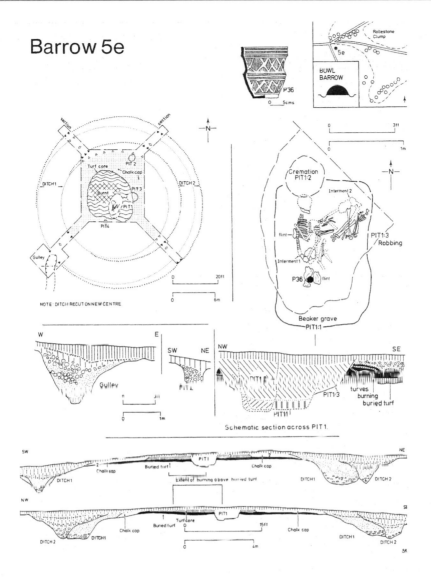

Barrow 5e

5 *Shrewton bowl barrow 5e, Wiltshire, drawn by Stephen Rollo-Smith*
(©: The Prehistoric Society)

hachure planning, to illustrate the often complex results of analytical survey in the field **(3)**.

The third strand of barrow enquiry is that of research and interpretation. The basis of many summaries and analyses is still the volumes of description and comment published by the nineteenth-century antiquarians, but in the twentieth century three key trends of thought can be identified. These can be viewed as turning points in the way that archaeologists thought about barrows — who built them, why they were built, and how they were used. The first key step forward was Stuart Piggott's definition of the Wessex Culture published in 1938. Drawing mainly on the results of the antiquarian excavations of Richard Colt Hoare, Piggott drew attention to the Early Bronze Age dating of a set of grave groups from round barrows, and discussed their possible social and political implications. The next major step occurred in the early 1970s when Fred Petersen developed the idea of multi-phased cemetery barrows, and Andrew Fleming showed how the mass of survey data compiled by Leslie Grinsell could be mapped and analysed to aid general social and economic interpretations. But barrows were still being thought of primarily as places for burying people. It was not until the late 1980s that a few archaeologists started to pull this idea apart and begin to write about funerals and barrow building in more human terms. These writings have centred on a consideration of how living human bodies moved around during the ceremonies associated with barrows, rather than the dead bodies that were placed in the graves. They talk about actors and audience, the building of facades and screens, the development of processional ways, and the erection of platforms for the enactment of rituals and displays. Finally, some writers have focussed more on the movements of people between barrows, patterns of pathways, and the importance of the views in and out from different sets of monuments.

Classifying barrows

In order to analyse and interpret large bodies of information, the human mind needs first to classify the data. This process involves defining categories. In the case of barrows, this means dividing the known barrows into groups according to shape, width and length, height and composition. These categories can then be compared one with each other in terms of contents, date, location, and degree of clustering, and according to their patterning in the landscape. The most basic division is between long barrows, all of which belong to the Neolithic period, and round barrows. Although mainly constructed in the Bronze Age, some round barrows were built in the Neolithic, and some originated then but were enlarged during the Early Bronze Age (**76**). Long barrows are divided into two main groups — earthen and megalithic — depending on whether the chambers contained within them were constructed from timber or from large stones. Round barrows have traditionally been divided into five types, the names of which are largely self-explanatory: bowl, bell, disc, saucer and pond barrows. These categories apply mainly to upland areas of chalk and limestone, and were used by Grinsell throughout the compilation of his county gazetteers. For the ring ditches found in some of the major river valleys other classifications have been devised, and in the highland areas of Britain, the types of mainly stone-built mounds are much more varied. The basic forms of simple cairns, platform mounds, kerb cairns, ring cairns and rimmed platform cairns can occur in myriad shapes and sizes, as is well illustrated by some of the types defined in the survey of Bodmin Moor undertaken by the Royal Commission in conjunction with the Cornwall Archaeological Unit (**6** and **7**). In the light of such classifications, it is interesting to observe that the recent Royal Commission survey of sites in the Salisbury Plain Training Area has shown that the variety of barrow forms is far greater than the simple traditional five-fold system might imply. The degree of variation is indicated in figure **8**, where some of the profiles conform to the traditional categories of round barrow, but several more unfamiliar terms, such as broad barrow and cone barrow, have also been employed. This wider range of barrow shapes, noticeable especially on Salisbury Plain, was also appreciated by Colt Hoare, who, at the beginning of his volumes on *Ancient Wiltshire*, includes engravings of no less than ten specific types of round barrow.

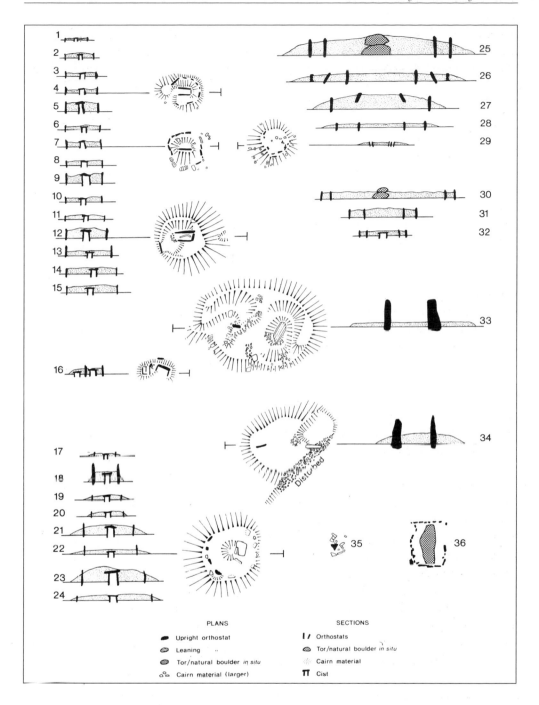

6 *Cairns on Bodmin Moor. 1-15 kerbed with cist, 16 with adjacent cist, 17-24 internal kerb with cist, 25-29 multiple internal kerbs, 30-32 multiple kerbs, 33-34 platforms with standing stones, 35 standing stone with stone setting around it, 36 grounder (earthfast boulder) with kerb. Vertical scale x 2.*
(© Crown copyright. NMR and © Cornwall Archaeological Unit)

17

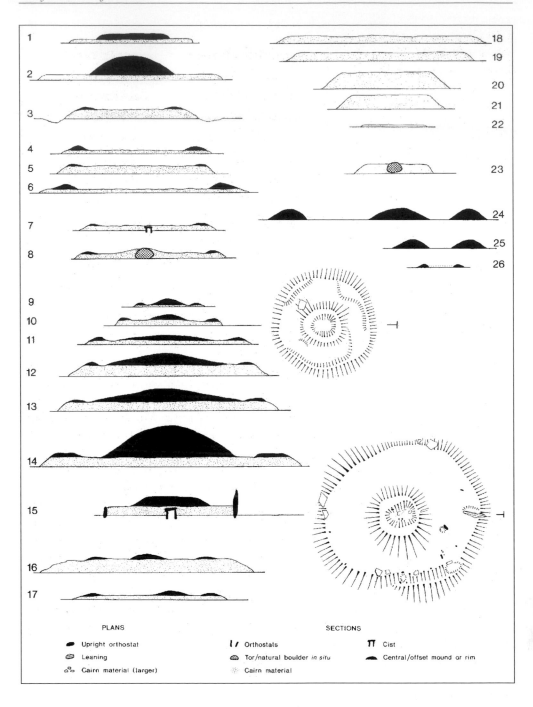

7 *Cairns on Bodmin Moor. 1-2 platform with central mound, 3-8 rimmed platform, 9-14 rimmed platform with central mound, 15 kerbed, standing stone, central mound, cist, 16-17, other rimmed platforms, 18-23 platforms, 24-26 ring cairns. Vertical scale x 2.*
(© Crown copyright. NMR and © Cornwall Archaeological Unit)

8 *Profiles of round barrows on Salisbury Plain. A-F bell barrows, G-I cone barrows, J-L bowl barrows, M-S broad barrows, T saucer barrow, U-V pond barrows, W-X disc barrows.*
(© Crown copyright. NMR)

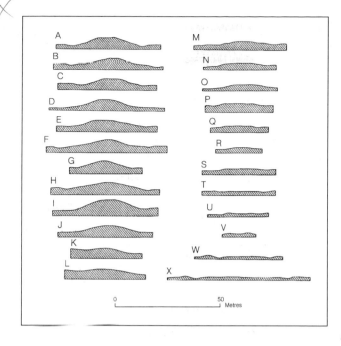

On the chalk, many barrow cemeteries or smaller groupings include only the simple mounds known as bowl barrows, but within this category there may be much discernible variation. Taking one small cemetery as an example, a group of bowl barrows situated on the side of the Till valley just north of Winterbourne Stoke village in Wiltshire (**colour plate 3**), such variation may be explored. It can immediately be seen that the barrows vary greatly in size and impact, and that some are distinctly flatter in profile than others. Some have distinct ditches around them while others do not, and at least one possesses a slight external bank. As all the barrows were dug into by Colt Hoare, we know the nature of some of the graves that lay beneath and within the mounds. From this information we can guess that the second largest mound, on the right of the picture, was a multi-phased monument, but the largest one probably was not. The finds from some of the mounds in the row of smaller contiguous barrows included cremations and pottery some of which may have been of a later date than the burials found in the larger barrows. But the dispersed outlying barrows, which are also the smallest and flattest, produced no burials at all. The entire group is surrounded by a continuous bank and ditch. Grinsell thought this to be of medieval date, but, whenever it was built, its purpose must have been to reserve the area of the barrows, and to keep them separate from animals, people or other kinds of land use. Such long term veneration of barrow land is a theme that will occur again in later chapters.

Barrow themes

This book is not a general textbook on prehistoric barrows. It is more one person's view of how barrows fit into the wider subject of British prehistory. We shall begin, in the next chapter, by looking at types of barrow and how they developed through time. There will also be consideration of grave goods, concentrating on the information that they can provide concerning social, economic and ritual arrangements. This will be developed further in

19

chapter 5 with a preliminary reassessment of the grave groups which are traditionally associated with the Wessex Culture of the Early Bronze Age. Chapters 3 and 4 will discuss other themes: how barrows relate to everyday activities at the local level, such as camp sites, settlements, fields and tracks; and how barrows were grouped together to form cemeteries. Finally, the last chapter will discuss how barrows acted as architectural markers and symbols in the wider landscape.

Running through all the chapters there will be two more general themes. The first is the idea of complexity. We have already encountered the difficulties of defining simple classifications of barrow type. Similar difficulties apply to the way individual mounds developed; many were multi-phased and were built, used, modified and extended over long periods of time. The same applies to cemeteries. Groups and arrangements of barrows often developed over many centuries and the ceremonies enacted at or amongst the barrows will no doubt have varied at different times. Lastly, the locations of barrows display infinite variety. On this topic, it is difficult to make any wide-ranging generalisations; we are still at the stage where barrows and groups of barrows need to be studied and analysed in detail within their local settings.

The second major theme is that of context, and this works at three main levels. On the smallest scale, study has concentrated on how objects were placed and grouped in the graves, or the layers of the mounds, and whether they appeared to be in mint condition, or were worn and possibly broken. Then there is close consideration of how mounds relate to other barrows, either within a cemetery or in more widely spaced groups, and how they relate to contemporary settlements, fields, boundaries and later land use. At the widest level, contextual analysis involves studies of how barrows were articulated into wider topographical settings and landscapes. To achieve these three aims, many excavation reports have been summarised, many barrows visited and museum collections scoured. Making the book has involved a great deal of reading, a lot of looking, and extensive walking. To begin to understand how prehistoric barrows worked it is necessary to put your own body into the surviving landscape, and also to confront the objects that were placed in the barrows, even if today there is a sheet of plate glass in between.

Notes

So as not to interrupt the flow of the book, references to other works have not been inserted in the text. Instead such references, and the details of any quotations, are included in a set of notes at the end of each chapter. These notes refer to the references, which may be found at the end of the book. For the same reason there are no references to calendar dates. To set the time periods in a calendar framework a simplified time chart is provided, again towards the end of the book, on page 145 (**76**).

Discussion of the legend of the Wayland Smith can be found in Grinsell 1976, 46-7 and 149. For an account of antiquarian excavators, see Marsden 1999. The key works by Fred Petersen and Andrew Fleming are Petersen 1972 and Fleming 1971. For a good presentation of the modern writings see Barrett 1994, and for a much earlier airing of some similar ideas see Fox 1959. The best textbooks on barrows are the brief introductions by Grinsell 1990 and Lynch 1997 and the more detailed treatments by Ashbee 1960 and 1970, and Kinnes 1979 and 1992.

2 Barrows as graves

One of the primary purposes of a barrow in prehistory was for the burial of one or more dead human bodies. Many mounds were constructed to cover and commemorate individuals or groups, and such mounds were often enlarged or heightened at later dates. Such aggrandisement was linked to the burying of further bodies, and others were frequently inserted into the tops or edges of existing barrows, or were buried on flat ground in between mounds or in the vicinity of barrow cemeteries. The main evidence for such burials is the bones of the bodies themselves, linked to the objects which may be found in association with the human remains.

In the past, most studies of grave goods have centred on aspects of relative chronology and dating. This is of crucial importance as it is on such analyses, amplified by the available absolute dates obtained from radiocarbon determinations, that the entire sequence of barrow and burial types has been based. A summary outline of this sequence is shown in the time chart (page 115). In most studies grave goods have been considered according to their raw material. For instance, gold objects, amber, bronzes and pottery have each been researched by different specialists, and there have been fewer general studies which combine the results to discuss the meaning of grave groups *as* groups. In fact, these groups of objects can provide a great deal of information concerning social matters, gender profiles, tool-kits and social or specialist status amongst the people who were buried, and those who were burying them. It is aspects such as these that will be emphasised here in the unfolding of a narrative that will cover the development of barrow burial from the early Neolithic through to the Iron Age period.

The bodies themselves can also provide a wealth of information concerning age, sex, traces of ancient disease, evidence for stature and health, as well as pointers to degrees of kinship affiliation or relatedness. Modern methods of analysis include basic visual identification of bones augmented by a battery of scientific techniques such as trace element and stable isotope analysis, or DNA analysis and blood-typing. However, techniques such as these can only be applied to human remains from recent excavations or, sometimes, on material that has been curated in museum collections. More information can be gained from the study of skeletons than from the remains of cremated bodies. Although techniques for the analysis and identification of cremations are highly refined, the information gained will always be more limited — basically the number of individuals represented, their ages, sex in certain cases, and, perhaps, aspects of the cremation process. Cremation was a popular funerary rite during many periods of prehistory, and our overall knowledge of human populations is much depleted as a result.

Another general problem is that most barrow excavations have not taken place in modern times. Although significant numbers of ploughed barrows were rescued by

9 *Excavation by H. St George Gray of a barrow at Winterborne Monkton, Dorset.* (© Crown copyright. NMR)

excavation in the twentieth century, many of the excavations took place prior to the major developments in scientific and environmental analysis that have occurred since about 1960 (**9**). Even worse, most of the upstanding barrows that have been excavated are those that were explored by antiquarians in the nineteenth century or earlier. In many cases, objects have been lost or were discarded or broken at the time of discovery. The human remains themselves suffered even more. Some barrow diggers, such as Canon Greenwell, retained the bones and produced anatomical reports that discussed the age, sex and stature of the people represented, but others left the bones or cremated remains in the excavation trenches and made no records at all. Unfortunately, the excavation of most of the major barrow cemeteries in Wessex, by Sir Richard Colt Hoare and William Cunnington, fell into the latter category. By comparison, the best antiquarian record, taking into account both objects and human bodies, relates to barrows on the Yorkshire Wolds.

Cemetery barrows
Many reports on barrow excavations and more general studies have described Neolithic and Bronze Age burials in terms of where they were located, both spatially and vertically, within the barrow. The main terms used are primary burial (under the centre of the mound), satellite burials and secondary burials. These descriptions were employed extensively by Leslie Grinsell in his published lists of the barrows from most of the counties of southern England. Over the years it became accepted that a primary burial was not only the original stimulus for the building of the barrow, but that this burial was also the most important. There can be little doubt that such an implication was by no means Grinsell's intention, but the idea that single, central inhumations beneath round barrows represented the norm for the Early Bronze Age at least has prevailed. Taking barrow 5L in the Shrewton group as an example, the labelling of the burials by the excavator, the late

Charles Green, can be compared with a modern analysis of the site (**10**). Green identified Pit 1 as the central primary burial, which had been robbed out to leave only fragments of an urn and cremated bone, Pit 2 as containing a rich secondary burial, and Interment 3 as a satellite burial. In contrast, Stephen Rollo-Smith's description defined seven different episodes of Bronze Age activity, with all the burial pits probably having been dug before the mound was raised. Recent research has attempted to correct the balance and to emphasise the progressive growth represented by the complex excavated evidence from certain barrows. However, the key work on this aspect was published as long ago as 1972 by Fred Petersen. This work has not been given the attention that it deserves and so will be summarised briefly at this stage.

Petersen pointed out that the emphasis on an Early Bronze Age single primary burial tradition partly derived from over-dependence on the results of the relatively poorly recorded antiquarian excavations from southern England. In Derbyshire and Yorkshire, the work of Bateman, Greenwell and Mortimer was generally recorded in more detail. From their descriptions it is possible to prove that many burials which would be described as 'satellites' in the Grinsell terminology were in fact all primaries beneath a single mound. Furthermore the central so-called 'primary' grave often contained the remains of several bodies, some complete and some incomplete. Multiple burials in a single grave often resulted from the deliberate re-opening of filled graves in order to insert further bodies, and this often led to the disturbance, either intentional or accidental, of earlier burials already in the grave. There are 70 examples of such graves in 66 barrows on the Yorkshire Wolds. All age grades from newborn to elderly are represented, although sub-adults may be under-represented. The burials of men and women occur roughly in equal proportions and it seems that such graves may have been used over fairly short periods, say a few generations, by extended families or other small kin units. For instance, in barrow 62 at Rudston, Yorkshire, the multiple grave included one elderly male, three other adult men, two adult women, two children and two infants. Similar grave deposits occur in Derbyshire, such as at Bee Low where a central stone cist contained seven partly or wholly disarticulated skeletons and a crushed Beaker pot. Traces of this multiple burial tradition are also known from a few of the better recorded sites in Wessex. One such site is Winterborne St Martin G46, on the South Dorset Ridgeway, where the central grave contained four complete skeletons and the disarticulated fragments of several others. There was evidence that the grave had been re-opened from the level of the surface of a primary flint cairn, and there was a cremation, with a dagger, nearby. This cremation seems to have been a separate deposit but, on the Yorkshire Wolds, remains of cremation and inhumation burials were found together in 23 instances. Thus it seems likely that particular families or social groups practiced the two rites contemporaneously. The thrust of Petersen's argument was that the so-called 'primary' barrow burial is just the first stage in a long burial sequence intended from the outset. The different stages of barrow construction are specific events that marked the ending of one set of successive burials and the beginning of the next series, all in a more or less continuous process of barrow use. Such a sequence is well illustrated by the phases of mound construction within Amesbury barrow G71, Wiltshire, a sequence which was revived and discussed afresh by John Barrett in 1988.

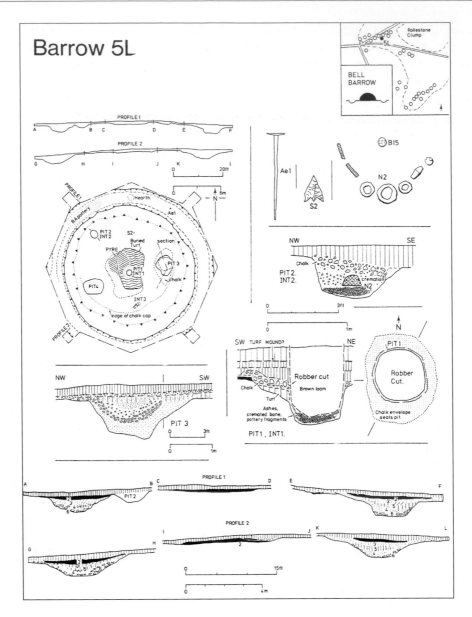

10 *Shrewton barrow 5L, Wiltshire.* (©: The Prehistoric Society)

Amesbury G71 was a large bell barrow set on the lower slopes of Beacon Hill where it overlooked the shallow basin within which Stonehenge is located. It was totally excavated by Patricia Christie and a full report was published in 1967. Barrett's scheme of phasing defines four main periods of construction. A primary grave, probably containing an adult skeleton, was set within a semi-circular setting of stakes and a small ring ditch. The grave was then re-cut much more deeply to receive the body of an adult man. In the next phase a series of three circles of wooden stakes were constructed outside the ring ditch and the central grave may have been re-cut once again. After decay or removal of the stakes, the third phase was marked by the building of a turf mound, which in turn was covered in layers of flints and then chalk from a surrounding ditch. The mound was used as a platform through which at least six graves were cut. These burials included two adults, one adolescent, three children and a baby; two of them were accompanied by pottery vessels and one adult woman had a single stone bead. A burnt area in the centre of the platform may have been a cremation pyre. Eventually this was covered with a layer of chalk and soil which included three stone beads, fragments of a further pot, an unburnt piece of human skull and some cremated bone. The fourth phase was marked by the raising of a second, higher turf stack and the digging of a new ditch, which was both deeper and of a larger diameter than the previous one. The turf mound was capped with chalk, and through this were inserted a cremation under a Collared Urn, an adult skeleton, and a cremation plus a bronze razor underneath another inverted urn. When the ditch had silted in part, graves were also inserted into the ditch filling. They included inhumations of one adult man, one adolescent and a child and there were also a series of cremations clustered in the south-east sector of the ditch silts. These represented four adults, a child and an infant, three of them buried with urns of Middle Bronze Age style.

This barrow is a prime example of an Early and Middle Bronze Age cemetery barrow. The funerary and ritual activities that were enacted at this site seem to have been linked to ancestral rites over many generations. Initially the central grave was the key focus and it was recut on several occasions. But as the barrow was raised and heightened through time the focus shifted to the wider area of the mounded platform, the space between the mound and the ditch, and then to the ditch silting itself. Thus the edge of the monument apparently became more important than the centre, or perhaps the centre was regarded as a sacrosanct zone within which further burial was not permitted. Also by this last phase of use, dated in part by the vessels to the Middle Bronze Age, the practice of cremation had replaced the mixed inhumation and cremation rite of earlier times. Glimpses of similar complex biographies of barrow construction can be gained from many reports on excavations of other round barrows throughout the country. One such excavation is that carried out in 1991 by Charly French at Deeping St Nicholas in south Lincolnshire.

The barrow at Deeping St Nicholas, which had been ploughed almost flat, was sited on a low gravel promontory next to a relict water course in the Fenland of the lower Welland valley. It was excavated in advance of destruction by gravel quarrying. The earliest evidence of ritual activity was the construction, on open ground, of a trapezoidal timber structure measuring about 11m by 5m. This may have been a mortuary house used to store a human body or bodies prior to burial. The first burial was that of a child, 3-5 years old, laid in a coffin, the position of which was marked by a substantial post or totem pole. With the skeleton there was a mint-condition flint knife, dated to the Beaker period of the Early Bronze Age. It was located at the centre of a series of up to nine concentric rings of wooden stakes (**11a**), and a shallow surrounding ditch, which may not have been continuous. The arrangement of stakes would have acted as a 'forest' of poles impeding access and view of the grave, except along prescribed lines of approach. After a period of 25-75 years, by which time the stakes had fallen or rotted away, the first barrow mound was constructed (**11b**). This mound, 20m in diameter, was built from turfs and topsoil and

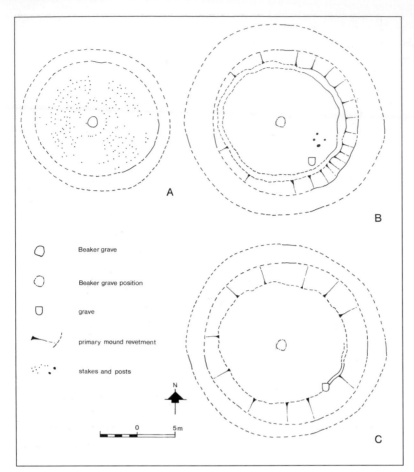

11 *The cemetery barrow at Deeping St Nicholas, Lincolnshire: phases A to C.* (after French)

○ Beaker grave

○ Beaker grave position

◡ grave

◥─╴ primary mound revetment

∴˙ ˙• stakes and posts

N

0   5m

A

B

C

capped with gravel taken from a substantial surrounding ditch. No burial was associated with the mound, and the excavator suggested that the barrow may have been intended as a memorial for the child buried earlier. Slightly later on, a continuous trench for timbers was cut through the outer edge of the mound, and the crouched skeleton of a woman was interred in a grave cut through the southeast sector of the primary mound (**11b**). Just northeast of the grave was a setting of four postholes that may have supported a small mortuary structure. The woman was in her twenties or thirties at the time of death and was buried with a string of four jet beads and a polished pig's tusk; the body was wrapped in a shroud or clothing. Within memory of the burial of this woman, the south-east sector of the timber palisade was removed and a further burial was inserted next to the female grave, but just to the south-east of it (**11c**). This was a man who had been 1.74m tall and his left lower arm bone showed evidence of a healed fracture; there were no grave goods with him. The excavator noted that 'considerable effort had gone into "breaking into the sanctity" of the area enclosed by the post circle of the first barrow and female inhumation. Yet interestingly, the internal space was not 'violated' as the male body was interred to the outside of the other burials and on the perimeter of the existing monument. One cannot help but speculate that the woman and the man were related....'

12 *The cemetery barrow at Deeping St Nicholas, Lincolnshire: phase D.* (after French)

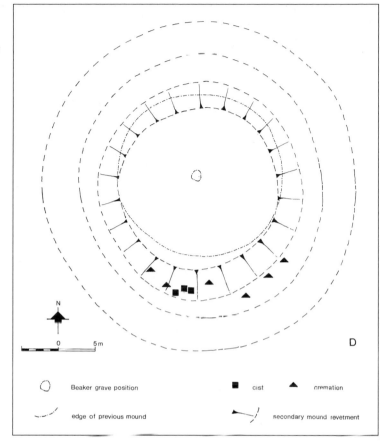

Beaker grave position   ■ cist   ▲ cremation

edge of previous mound   secondary mound revetment

After a short period of time, probably less than ten years, the ditch had partly silted up. At this point the barrow was completely remodelled. The second mound was a medium-sized bell barrow, centred slightly to the south-east of the first barrow and surrounded by a new and much larger ditch (**12d**). Built into the gravel mound revetment on the south-west side, two slab stone cists were built. Each cist covered at least one cremation in a pit, and outside each one there was another cremation contained in a Middle Bronze Age urn, one of which may have been in a third cist. The burials inside the well-preserved cists were of adults and each urn contained the remains of an immature person. None of these burials overlapped each other, indicating that the location of each grave was remembered by the community, or marked in some way. Finally, a series of six to ten cremations were interred in six small pits on the berm of the second barrow, in the south-west and south-east sectors. One was a double cremation, one triple and one was placed with a pot, which was lined with several sherds from a small decorated vessel of Middle Bronze Age type. Adults and children were represented. Charred plant remains recovered from the cremation deposits suggested that at this time the area around the barrow was grassland and that there were areas of trampled earth in the vicinity. The pyre was fuelled with species from woodland and scrub as well as some from the fen environment. Grasses and herbs may have been employed as kindling. By this time the groundwater level was rising and, by the later Bronze Age, the barrow had been engulfed by peat.

The sequence at Deeping St Nicholas can be divided into seven main phases of activity: the pre-barrow mortuary house, the child's grave surrounded by its 'forest' of stakes, the first barrow mound and its ditch, the palisade trench and the rich female burial, the partial demolition of the palisade and insertion of the male grave, the building of the larger bell barrow and its ditch, the interment of cremations in the two cists and cremations outside them and, finally, the insertion of six cremation pits on the south-east sector of the berm. On radiocarbon evidence this sequence lasted about 500 years, which, taking a Bronze Age generation to have been in the order of 25 years, is about 20 generations. The first three inhumation graves, the cist burials and the cremations in the south-east sector are discrete groups each of which may well have belonged to single families or close social groups, and it is not impossible that all three groups of burials belonged to a single local community which had used the barrow over half a millennium. However, the excavator felt that the deliberate placing of the cist burials in the south-west sector, away from the man and the woman buried further to the east, may indicate that these cremated individuals were from a different, but possibly related, community. The same divergence might apply to the two groups of later cremations — one in the south-west sector and the other to the south-east.

Long barrows

Having established the principle of the complexity of barrow construction and the concept of the 'cemetery barrow', we shall now begin to look at a series of different types of barrow, considering them in roughly chronological order. Neolithic long barrows were usually built using material dug from two flanking ditches (**13**). The mounds were often higher, and wider, at one end. It was here that any burials were generally placed and where ceremonies were performed. Individual barrows vary greatly in size and exact shape; field survey can reveal structural detail, evidence of damage and relationships with later features. However, knowledge of interior structure, and of any burials and objects deposited within the barrows, must come from excavation.

Thus, we shall turn to consider two earthen long barrows in the Wessex region, both of which have been extensively excavated, prior to destruction by ploughing, to reveal the remains of timber mortuary houses beneath them. The first was at Nutbane on the Hampshire chalk. This was excavated by Faith Morgan in 1957 (**14**). The plan shows that the western end of the mound area and the two straight flanking ditches were investigated in selective trenches, but the eastern end of the mound was totally excavated. The first structure to have been built was the small sub-rectangular enclosure below letter m on the plan plus four post pits in front of it to the east. The pits probably held the posts of a wooden mortuary house, in front of the small chamber, which had also been of timber, with sloping sides like a tent. Inside this there were two crouched male skeletons, placed on their left with heads to the east, and to the west of them a crouched skeleton of a child laid on its right with head to the south. The bones were weathered and slightly disarranged. Then the mortuary house was rebuilt on a much larger scale, producing an impressive 'forecourt' structure with flanking facades, the foundations of which are indicated on the plan (**14**, f). A few plain

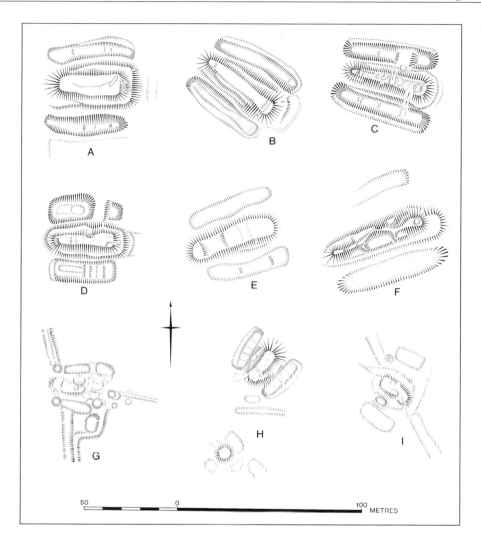

13 *Long barrows on Salisbury Plain: A. Ell Barrow; B. East Down, the position of an excavation trench at the south-east end; C. Norton Bavant, a series of excavation trenches on the summit; D. Boles Barrow; E. Netheravon 6; F. Tinhead, partly quarried for chalk; G. Knook Down, disfigured by shell fire. It is a focus for linear earthworks; H. Knook, a short example, and an adjacent round barrow; I. Imber Down is partly levelled and a focus for military activity.* (© Crown copyright. NMR)

Neolithic bowl sherds and animal bones were found here. The original timber burial chamber was dismantled, and the foundation ditches were backfilled. This important area was then redefined by a timber enclosure built in a 'log cabin' construction technique. Inside this were the remains of a further crouched male skeleton placed on his right with head to the south. The chamber was later infilled with chalk and earth, including more bowl sherds and animal bones. A mound was piled up around the log enclosure and then the 'forecourt'

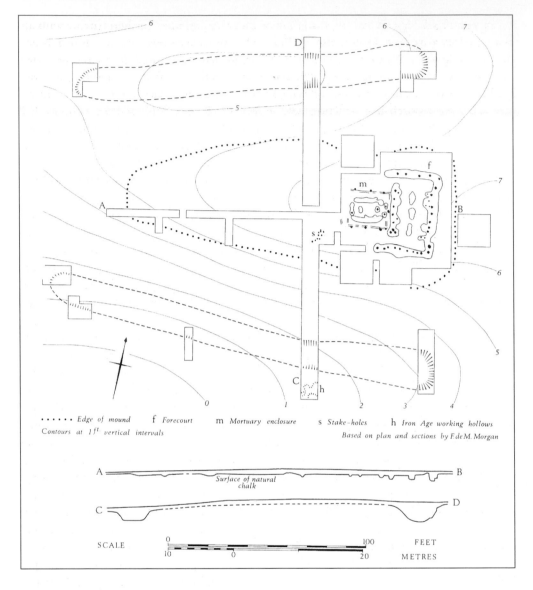

Edge of mound   f Forecourt   m Mortuary enclosure   s Stake-holes   h Iron Age working hollows

Contours at 1 ft vertical intervals   Based on plan and sections by F. de M. Morgan

14 *Plan and sections of the Nutbane earthen long barrow, Hampshire.*
(© Crown copyright. NMR)

building was set on fire. The long mound was then completed, incorporating within it more bowl sherds, flintwork and animal bones, while the skull of a man was set up above the mortuary house. The animal bones included remains of wild ox, sheep or goat, pig, red and roe deer. Part of a Beaker came from the upper filling of the south ditch — this may have come from a burial inserted into the long mound, but if it did, all traces of that burial had been destroyed by ploughing of the mound, which, on circumstantial evidence, can be said to have commenced in the Iron Age.

At Fussell's Lodge, Wiltshire, Paul Ashbee excavated another earthen barrow with an associated mortuary enclosure, also in 1957. The mortuary enclosure was much larger than those found at Nutbane and was trapezoidal in shape, its plan defining the area later occupied by the long mound itself. The enclosure was formed from closely set oak posts held in a narrow bedding trench and with an entrance at the wider, eastern end. Outside this there was a porch-like structure held in four small post-holes and the entrance led directly into a long, narrow burial chamber of tent-like construction. Within the chamber was a deposit of human bones resting on flint nodules above a layer of turf. The people represented were ten men, nine women, thirteen adults of unknown sex and twelve children, along with pottery, flintwork and three sets of lower front foot bones and tail bones from oxen. The human bones were all disarticulated and arranged deliberately in five groups along the axis of the chamber. Also there were two near-complete pots, one placed at each end of the burial chamber. A decorated vessel was associated with the bones from eleven adults and one child, while, at the entrance end, a small plain pot and an ox skull lay next to the bones of two women. In the filling material there were pieces from seven more bowls, six of them decorated, along with the bones from five adults and five children. Finally the flanking ditches were dug out and these provided material for the main barrow mound.

In comparison with this wealth of burial information, it is instructive next to consider a long barrow that produced no direct evidence of burials at all. At South Street, near Avebury, Isobel Smith excavated the entire mound and eight major sections across the flanking ditches of another trapezoidal earthen long barrow. The ground surface beneath the mound showed traces from criss-cross ploughing with a simple ard, although immediately prior to construction the land seems to have been used as pasture. A group of sarsen stones had then been gathered together roughly near the site of the eastern end of the later mound. Then a framework of stakes and hurdles was constructed, forming a sequence of twenty paired bays along the site axis. A large sarsen was added to the existing ones and the bays filled, in order from the east end, with turf, chalk and soil. The only finds were animal bones and antler fragments in the ditches, and worked bone and antler fragments from the mound. Many archaeologists, working within a framework which involved interpretation of long barrows as primarily funerary monuments, have been puzzled by the lack of burial remains here, and have suggested that it was a cenotaph barrow, erected in memory of one or more persons whose bodies were not available for burial. However, the theme of this book stresses the need to work out the multiple functions and symbolism of barrows — burial is only one such function and it should be no surprise to discover that sometimes other uses, such as those connected to territoriality or community consciousness, were paramount. Such ideas as these will be discussed further in the next chapter.

Before turning to some megalithic tombs, it will be useful to consider the evidence from one more earthen long barrow. This example is from the north-east where, in Lincolnshire and Yorkshire, a series of long barrows display some rather different features. The barrow on Willerby Wold was excavated in part by Canon Greenwell in 1865 and more fully by Terry Manby between 1958 and 1960. Initially there was a trapezoidal mortuary enclosure, with continuous timber posts set in a concave façade with a central

15 *Stone chambered long barrow at Belas Knap, Gloucestershire. Viewed from the north-east in 1982.* (© Crown copyright. NMR)

pit and timber slots down the sides. Behind the façade was a banked chamber with a central pit. There were some disarticulated bones, including three skulls. The timber façade was then burnt and the chamber filled in with chalk and flint chunks which were interlaced with timber and sealed over with turf. The ditches were then dug to provide material for the mound, and a few sherds of plain bowls were deposited in the bottom of the ditch. Then, and this is the process that is different, the filled chamber was set on fire from the east end. The chamber thus acted as a crematorium, with temperatures having reached 1200°C.

More well known to visitors of archaeological monuments are the long barrows constructed from stone and which incorporate megalithic burial chambers. These are most common in Wales, Ireland and Scotland, but there is an important and accessible set in south Wales and on the Cotswolds, known as the Cotswold-Severn group. One of the best preserved of these limestone mounds is that at Belas Knap in Gloucestershire (**15**). This splendid example contains four burial chambers and a false entrance (**colour plate 4**). The four chambers include one at the south end (left on **15**), one at the midway point on each of the long sides of the barrow, and another set halfway between the eastern chamber and the south end. Parts of the barrow were excavated in 1863-5 and 1928-31. There is some evidence to suggest that each of the four chambers was contained in a separate mound prior to the construction of the large trapezoidal mound. If this were so then the largest feature of the barrow, the false entrance at the northern end, was also the latest. This entrance was formed by two portal stones, a lintel and a large blocking slab. Its forecourt was defined by carefully laid drystone walling which supported two convex horn-shaped projections. The burial chambers contained bones from about thirty people, while a male skull and bones from five children had been placed behind the blocking stone of the false entrance. This false entrance may have been designed in part to confuse potential tomb robbers. Interestingly, the Cotswold-Severn tombs also display some other techniques of constriction and concealment, such as burial passage entrances almost blocked by stones, or the deliberated addition of extra stone revetment material which was built across the entrances to some of the chambers. This aspect of rendering elements of the tomb secret and hidden may have involved strong symbolic overtones as well as the functional protection of the human remains contained within.

Discussions of burial within megalithic long barrows most often centre on the spectacular finds from the West Kennet long barrow which were published so elegantly by Stuart Piggott. However, many aspects of those deposits, and the later filling of the tomb, are exotic and unusual, and it seems better here to concentrate on a lesser known, and perhaps more typical, example. Pant-y-Saer is a kidney-shaped stone cairn on Anglesey; it was totally excavated by Sir Lindsay Scott in 1933. The cairn has a concave forecourt facing north and a complex of internal walls, with a roughly central rectangular megalith chamber constructed over a rectangular pit. From the forecourt area, and especially against the north stone of the chamber, came some groups of bone, both human and animal, bowl sherds and some worked stone objects. These finds may have come originally from the chamber which was dug out during a previous excavation of 1875. Still in the chamber were four flint scrapers and scrapers, while the substantial part of a Beaker, found on a rock ledge at the side of the chamber, probably was that known to have been found with a burial in an intrusive stone cist discovered during the 1875 campaign.

In addition to this brief outline of the contents of a fairly typical megalithic tomb, it is useful to consider the summary of finds from all the excavated tombs of north Wales compiled by Frances Lynch. This is summarised in figure **16**, alongside a similar, but less detailed, analysis of the material from the Cotswold-Severn megalithic barrows. It can be noted that the types of material present, and their relative proportions, are remarkably similar for the two groups of tombs. On the whole, artefacts are sparse, and when they do

Finds	North Wales	Cotswold-Severn region
human remains	8	12
animal remains	7	8
Early Neolithic pottery	6	8
Beaker pottery	4	4
flint	9	7
stone	1	1
bone pin	3	-
pendant or bead	2	-
shells	6	-
white quartz	5	-

16 *Numbers of finds from nine megalithic tombs in north Wales and fifteen in the Cotswold-Severn region.* (after Lynch and Darvill)

occur they are of common materials — pottery, flint and stone. Exotic items are very rare, although the shells and pieces of white quartz are important items and their potential significance of such pieces will be explored further in Chapter 5. With the sorts of finds from megalithic tombs in mind, we may return now to a summary of the finds made in the earthen long barrows (**17**). Again, the most common classes of find, after human remains, are sherds of bowl pottery and animal bones, followed by flint points and tools. Overall, finds from Neolithic long barrows are rather uncommon, quite varied and superficially not very spectacular. Few items, maybe only the flint arrowheads, can be linked to particular individuals, and these are men in cases where sex can be determined. However at least some of them were found embedded in portions of the skeleton and may have been the cause of death rather than deposited deliberately with the body. Many other arrowheads are broken. Other flintwork sometimes includes groups of knapped material, such as a core plus fitting flakes, and these, plus the relatively common occurrence of plain pottery, may signify the small social group rather than the individual. Most pots are

	bowl	flint point	flint or stone tool	various	ox skull	ox feet	antler pick	animal bone
primary associations	16	11	15	slider bead decorated stone	4	4	-	7
indirect primary associations	38	1	35	-	3	-	12	18

17 *Finds from early Neolithic long barrows: figures denote numbers of sites, not numbers of objects.* (after Kinnes)

represented by only a few sherds, and it may be that these were brought in from a distant activity site or midden. In a few cases, as at Fussell's Lodge, whole pots were placed next to the bone heaps and, in some Yorkshire sites, substantial portions of vessels were found from the area of the façade trenches. These may have been deposited deliberately during ceremonies held in the forecourt. Of particular interest are the skulls and foot bones from wild oxen or cattle. These are probably the surviving elements from leather hides, the so-called 'head and hoof' deposits, which also occur, sporadically, in some Early Bronze Age round barrows. Some single skulls however were placed deliberately, as at Beckhampton Road, Wiltshire, where three ox skulls lay at points along the length of the mound and one may have been displayed on a wooden post. In secondary deposits within earthen long barrows, usually in the flanking ditches, pottery and flint knapping debris are by far the most common categories (**17**). These, and animal bones, often occur in distinct clusters, and more exotic items such as ox skulls and carved chalk objects have occasionally been found as well. These are examples of structured deposition — the deliberate selection and placing of cultural materials in different contexts for symbolic reasons. This is an important concept discussed and defined by Julian Thomas in his book *Understanding the Neolithic*.

Finally, we need to think a little more about the bones and the bodies. Most of the bodies found in long barrows are disarticulated and incomplete. There are a few whole skeletons and, rarely, cremations. Unfortunately, many long barrows were excavated during the nineteenth century so we cannot rely too heavily on published estimates of the number and sex of the people represented, or on accounts of the detailed arrangements of the bones beneath the barrows. However, some clear trends can be detected. For instance, the bones were often deposited in heaps, sometimes with the long bones in discrete bundles and the skulls arranged separately. Although, as we have seen above, at Nutbane there was a simple sequence of four inhumations, at Fussell's Lodge all the bones were disarticulated and occurred in discrete groups. The contents and arrangement of these groups are summarised in figure **18**. One especially interesting aspect of such bone deposits is that different parts of the body are not evenly represented. At Fussell's Lodge small bones such as ribs, vertebrae, and those from hands and feet, are relatively

location	male	female	adult	child	long bones	skulls
NW	1	1	1	1	laid axially	at sides
SW	2	1	3	-	laid axially	at sides
W of centre	5	3	3	11	laid transversely	dispersed
E of centre	-	2	-	-	laid diagonally	single skull
E	-	2	-	-	laid diagonally	single skull
totals	10	9	13	12		

18 *The composition of five bone groups within the Fussell's Lodge burial chamber.* (after Kinnes)

uncommon, and long bones are also under-represented. On the other hand, there are relatively large numbers of skulls or skull fragments. These observations, plus the high degree of weathering of the bones recorded on many sites, suggest that the dead bodies had been exposed, either on platforms or within secure enclosures (as shown at Hambledon Hill in Dorset), or had been buried initially elsewhere. The bones had later been retrieved or dug up and brought to the long barrow for subsequent interment. However, of the larger bones certain types seem to have been retrieved more often than others. In the area around Avebury, it has been noted that some of the human bone types that are apparently 'missing' from the long barrow burial chambers occur in the ditches of the adjacent ceremonial enclosure on Windmill Hill. This may mean that certain bones were selected as representing particular groups or individuals and were subsequently circulated amongst the living as relics. At Fussell's Lodge, children and adolescents are severely under-represented but the balance of male to female seems about right. Some of the bone groups contained a higher proportion of children (figure 18: W of centre), or females only (E of centre and E), but the statistical testing of the significance of such patterns must await the future excavation of further large bone deposits.

Whether all the bone deposits on any one site were contemporary cannot be determined at present. Many sites display long structural sequences — mortuary houses rebuilt, and chambers replaced — but the time-scale within which these changes took place is not known. It could be anything between less than one year and several centuries. From the finds and the human remains we may conclude that long barrows were to do with human groups rather than individuals, and that the cultural deposits may have reflected everyday tasks, such as tool production, hunting or food preparation, as well as communal activities such as feasting. But altogether the overriding impression is of the movement of materials: a flint core from flint source to base camp to long barrow ditch; a pot from home production site to seasonal feast to forecourt ceremony and bone heap; and human leg bone from flat grave or excarnation enclosure to a long bone bundle in a tomb, wooden chamber or crematorium.

Round barrows

From the later Neolithic period, the story begins to change. Barrows reflect less the communal aspect of human life and death. New rites seem to involve individual men, women and children: clues are held in the form of the barrows themselves, now both large and round, and in the types and numbers of grave goods. In an important study of Neolithic round barrows and ring ditches, Ian Kinnes was able to show that round barrows did not occur first in the late Neolithic to Early Bronze Age Beaker period, but had been present from the early Neolithic. Some were contemporary with long barrows but many more are dated a little later, when they became the main barrow type of the later Neolithic. The human remains found within Neolithic round barrows are usually single complete skeletons — a significant departure from the groups of disarticulated bones from beneath long barrows. However, it must be remembered that some long barrows also covered single inhumation burials only. By careful analysis of the stratification and associations of different classes of grave goods, Kinnes was able to define a chronological sequence of burial types for the Neolithic round barrows. In the earlier stages there were crematoria, particularly prevalent in northern England and similar to the example from the Willerby Wold long barrow described above. The human remains are usually arranged in linear zones and occasionally, as at Swale's Tumulus in Suffolk, an actual pyre area lay beneath the mound. In the later stages there is a tendency for there to be more individual burials (75% of recorded examples) and the grave goods seem to emphasise personal status. The single burials are often contained in specific graves or stone cists, and eventually there is evidence for a series of enclosed cremation cemeteries. However, although these are defined by ring ditches these are not really barrows. With burials of the earlier stages of Neolithic round barrow, associated finds include widespread types such as leaf arrowheads, but also new categories of object which seem to denote prestige or specific tool kits. Such objects are stone rubbers and pounders and boar's tusk blades. In the later stages this trend becomes very much more obvious. There are a series of flint and stone items which have been flaked, ground and polished to a very high degree of workmanship, in fact to a degree far beyond any functional requirements: edge-polished flint axes, polished plano-convex knives and lozenge arrowheads alongside specialised antler maceheads, which may have been symbolic emblems for display, and, as in the earlier series, boar's tusk blades. The developmental sequence is especially well illustrated by the succession of burials found under the massive round mound at Duggleby Howe in Yorkshire.

Deriving from this insular round barrow tradition of the later Neolithic, and also influenced by developments in Europe, are the much smaller barrows of the Beaker period. Classic Beaker barrows were simple, small and round and often were surrounded by an interrupted ditch from which the mound material was obtained. As an example one can cite Grinsell's barrow 51 in Amesbury parish, which lies in the Cursus barrow group just northwest of Stonehenge. It was excavated by William Cunnington in 1805 and, due to continuing plough damage, by Paul Ashbee in 1960. A central rectangular grave was cut 1.7m into the chalk. It contained the remains of a mortuary house with squared corner timbers and a contracted male skeleton, probably associated with a fine decorated Beaker originally found by Cunnington. This was covered by a small mound of chalk rubble. Then the causewayed ditch was laid out and dug and the resulting turf, topsoil and chalk used to build a small barrow over the existing mound. A second tightly contracted burial was placed in a grave cut through the silts in the bottom of the ditch on the north-west side, and again the burial was associated with a finely decorated Beaker vessel. Somewhere towards the base of the mound Cunnington found another burial which was associated with yet another Beaker and traces of folded leather which may have been a hide. Finally, further burials were inserted into the crest of the barrow and two of these also had Beakers. One of these burials also had a set of leather worker's tools: a bronze awl with a protective antler cover, a flint scraper, a pointed roe-deer antler with a sheath and an antler spatula. The skull of the first burial had undergone a trephination — the surgical removal of a roundel of the cranium, intended to relieve pressure on the brain — and the large roundel had been replaced in the grave. This operation was probably the cause of death. A similar, but simpler, sequence of burials was found in barrow 5e on Net Down, Shrewton (**5**). Here there were two central contracted burials in deep pits, one with a decorated Beaker. Above these a simple barrow of turf and chalk was raised. Later on the ditch was re-dug and a new mound constructed, probably to contain an urn burial which originally occupied the smaller pit 1:2.

Although the burial rite represented in such Beaker barrows is that of single inhumation, many barrows contain successions of such burials. Often the locations of later and inserted burials imply that the exact positions of former graves were known. These may have been marked, but over longer periods of time it seems that a sophisticated tradition of group memory was in action. The existence of personalised groups of prestige goods noted with the later series of Neolithic round barrows is now very much in evidence. Such groups include exotic items as well as specific tool kits — for instance relating to flint- and stone-working, hunting, fire-making, or leather-working, as described above. The exotic items occur in very few burials but include the first copper knives, stone axe hammers, a few items of gold, shale or jet buttons and belt rings, and the very specific sets of archery equipment which include arrowheads and the highly polished flat or curved stone wristguards. The Beaker pots themselves are also very finely finished exotic items, and there is evidence that some of them at least were manufactured specifically for use in the grave. As well as sets of successive Beaker graves in round barrows, extensive excavation of some barrows in modern times has shown that sometimes groups of burials were interred. At West Overton barrow Grinsell 6b, Wiltshire, a crouched male skeleton with a Beaker was buried in an oval pit centrally placed within a stony bank, and there was also a cremation in the same pit. Around the pit were the shallow graves of five crouched children. Cutting one of these were two cremations in Early Bronze Age Collared Urns which also had been deposited before the barrow mound was constructed over all the burials.

At Barnack in Cambridgeshire a ploughed barrow, which survived as three concentric ring ditches, was excavated by Peter Donaldson. Although the remains were much damaged, a threefold sequence of construction was deduced (**19**). The excavator did not feel that the extensive series of burials could be put in any overall order, apart from the three sequential graves at the centre. However, using the stratigraphic evidence presented in the report, together with the seven radiocarbon dates obtained from various of the burials, the following integrated phasing for the barrow has been worked out. Firstly, a small ring ditch was constructed. This was quickly backfilled but not before a flexed infant skeleton and a plain Beaker had been deposited in the base. An adjacent flexed male skeleton with no grave goods produced a very early radiocarbon date and may have been a flat grave dug prior to the ring ditch itself. In the centre of the small ring ditch a deep shaft grave was dug, and in this lay the extended body of an adult man along with a very large and fine Beaker, a copper dagger, a unique pendant made from the ivory of a sperm whale or walrus and a very exotic green schist wristguard, with eighteen holes each of which was covered with a gold cap. Over this grave a primary mound was built, using material from a larger ditch laid out roughly concentrically around the backfilled inner ditch (*see* **19**). In phase 2, a second central burial, this time a cremation, was made in a grave cutting the top of the filling of the shaft grave, and another adjacent burial may, on radiocarbon evidence, have been roughly contemporary. Both were adult men. The existing mound was refurbished by the provision of timber stake revetments and further material taken from the second ditch. In the third phase, a third central male grave was inserted and at the same time or in subsequent years seven further graves were arranged around it. These included skeletons of five men, two women, one child and one newborn baby, mostly in a flexed or contracted position. The baby was found in the same grave as a man and the other double burial contained an extended man plus a flexed skeleton which was probably a woman. This last grave was the only one of this phase to have any associated finds: a bone point and three flint scrapers. All the burials were interred most probably before the erection of the final and largest mound — a bell barrow seemingly, with a large ditch and space for a berm between it and the site of the barrow itself (*see* **19**). There were traces of four more plough-damaged burials and two which cannot be assigned to any particular constructional phase. One of these was an infant of three months buried with a small pot of Early Bronze Age Food Vessel type.

19 *Barnack, Cambridgeshie: suggested development of the barrow.* (after Donaldson)

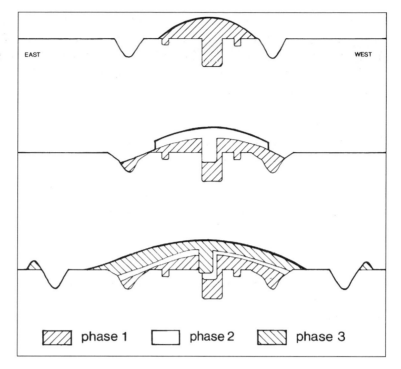

Popular perception of the rich graves of Early Bronze Age date, those commonly described as belonging to a Wessex Culture, has been influenced largely by the contents of the Bush Barrow burial. This burial, found beneath one of the most prominent round barrows in the vicinity of Stonehenge, was excavated by William Cunnington and Colt Hoare and contained some very famous rich grave goods including three daggers, an axe, two gold lozenge plates and the bone mounts and a polished fossil head from a handled mace or sceptre. This group of objects is in fact unique amongst the Wessex Culture grave assemblages, but they have given rise to the idea of a wealthy, male-dominated, warrior chiefdom which is deemed to have held sway in this area of southern England for several centuries. The exact nature of these grave assemblages is the main subject of a later chapter, but here it is necessary to consider a few Early Bronze Age barrows in order to explore the variety of rites employed. Firstly it is important to note that most burials under barrows were not accompanied by grave goods at all — they were simple cremations. The most common items to be found in graves of this date are flint flakes and pottery vessels, and by far the most widespread form of pot is the Collared Urn (**20**). Taking one of the fairly well known Wessex Culture cemeteries not far from Stonehenge, that located on Lake Down, it may be surprising to discover that of the eight barrows excavated by the Reverend Duke in the nineteenth century, only three produced any burials at all. These included one central cremation in a small urn, one off-centre cremation in a larger urn and two central unaccompanied cremations. There were no items of metal or other exotic substances. When one turns to some of the other rich 'Wessex' sites, the situation becomes even more complex, for, in several cases, there is no evidence that the rich objects were associated with human remains at all.

20 *Three Collared Urns from Bincombe Barrow G4, Dorset.* (© Dorset Natural History and Archaeological Society)

One of the most exotic groups of Early Bronze Age items from a barrow is the group from Clandon which is on display in the Dorset County Museum at Dorchester (**colour plate 5**). This very large bowl barrow, located on the same ridge as Maiden Castle, was excavated by Edward Cunnington in 1882 (**colour plate 22**). Owing to the loose nature of the mound material he did not reach the old ground surface below the mound, or any primary interment (**21**). The main Early Bronze Age feature investigated was a low cairn of flints found 7ft (2.1m) below the surface. Beneath this cairn were the scattered fragments of a miniature incense cup. These had been deposited on a bed of white clay before the flints were mounded up. On the southern edge of the cairn lay a dagger, which was broken and the wider end of which was apparently missing. Fragments of its wooden sheath were also noted. On the top of the cairn the incised gold lozenge, similar to that from Bush Barrow, had been placed, and near to it, a shale macehead, or head of a sceptre, embellished originally with five gold bosses. Finally, amongst the flints and over the cairn surface were the fragments of an amber cup. There were no human remains, burnt or unburnt. Some way above the flint cairn a human cremation was found, number 2 on figure **21**. This was found with a Collared Urn, which had been crushed flat on a thin layer of ashes and small flints. A little higher in the mound there were three successive layers of ash, and above these, two graves made from flat stones. These contained adult and juvenile skeletons that may have been Roman in date. As the height of the barrow was recorded as 18.5ft (5.6m), it is apparent that the rich Early Bronze Age items were deposited at a position less that halfway down within the barrow. In other words, they were the result of a rite held some

21 *Section
through the
Clandon Barrow,
drawn by Charles
Drew from
Edward
Cunnington's
original sketch.
(©: Dorset
Natural History
and
Archaeological
Society)*

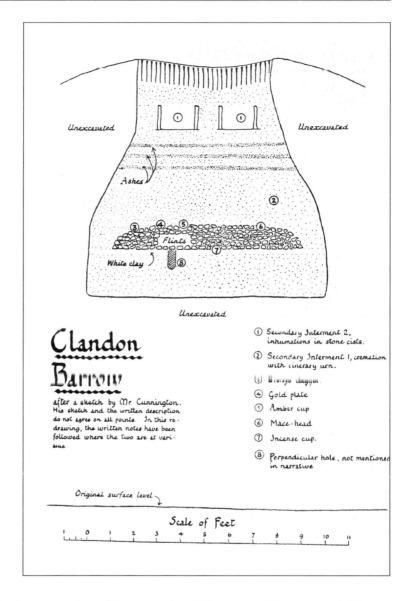

Clandon
Barrow

after a sketch by Mr. Cunnington.
His sketch and the written description
do not agree on all points. In this re-
drawing, the written notes have been
followed where the two are at vari-
ance.

① Secondary Interment 2,
   inhumations in stone cists.

② Secondary Interment 1, cremation
   with cinerary urn.

③ Bronze dagger.

④ Gold plate

⑤ Amber cup

⑥ Mace-head

⑦ Incense cup.

⑧ Perpendicular hole, not mentioned
   in narrative

Original surface level

Scale of Feet

time after the original construction of the mound, which may well have started life as a
Neolithic or Beaker round barrow. Furthermore, this rite did not involve the deposition of
any human remains.

Another find not directly associated with a human body or cremation is the very rich
group of objects found in a modern excavation, the salvage of a ring ditch at Lockington in
Leicestershire, on the path of the Derby southern bypass in 1994 (**22**). The earliest feature
was a Neolithic pit which contained traces of cremated bone which may have been human.
This may have derived from a funeral pyre. The presence of this pit suggests that this
particular spot was special in some way long before the Bronze Age barrow was built. In
the Early Bronze Age a ring gully was constructed, probably to support a timber palisade
around a mortuary enclosure 38m in diameter. The main entrance was to the north. Inside

22 *View of the excavation of the Lockington barrow, Leicestershire*
(©: Gwilym Hughes, Birmingham University Field Archaeology Unit)

the enclosure there was no evidence of burning but a deposit of charcoal containing flecks of cremated bone seemed to be the remains of pyre material brought in from elsewhere. Scattered across the charcoal layer were a number of broken pieces of pottery from an Enlarged Food Vessel Urn. Analysis of the soils suggested that immediately prior to the deposition of the charcoal and pottery, and the building of the barrow mound, the enclosure may have been occupied by animals. This presence of personal or family wealth in the form of livestock may have been connected with the funerary rituals. At the same time, or probably rather earlier, a highly unusual selection of exotic items were deposited in a small pit dug at the entrance to the enclosure (**colour plate 6**). This is an important symbolic location, lying between the inside and the outside of the enclosed space. The objects include a very large copper dagger in its sheath, and two decorated ribbed bracelets in gold. Over these the fragmentary remains of two pots, both probably Beakers, had been deliberately placed. The dagger and bracelets are personal items normally found in graves rather than hoards. However, in this case no burial was present, and the objects seem to have been placed in the style of a hoard — in other words, with a view to them being retrieved at some later date. Such a view is reinforced by the finding of a stone slab decorated with cup marks in the ditch deposits nearby. This may have stood originally as a marker stone above the special deposit. The broken pots are an unusual find in such a context; they may have been heirlooms, imbued with strong ancestral power.

Further discussion of Early Bronze Age grave goods and their potential significance is reserved for chapter 5, but meanwhile the general chronological overview of barrow types and their contents will be continued by moving on to the quite different traditions of mound building and use that developed during the Middle Bronze Age period.

Round barrows, old and new

Although it is generally thought that most British round barrows date from the Early Bronze Age, many of them were re-used for burial in the Middle Bronze Age and a large number were still being constructed during that period. Most of the well-dated Middle Bronze Age burials come from southern England, where they are associated with particular forms of pottery belonging to the Deverel-Rimbury tradition. This is named after two sites in Dorset — one is The Deverel Barrow (**23**), and the other a flat cremation cemetery at Rimbury near Weymouth. Although a fair number of cremation cemeteries are known, the interment of burials within round barrows continued to be by far the most common practice. Newly built barrows tended to be smaller in size than the preceding round barrows of the Early Bronze Age and where earlier barrows were selected for re-use it was the simple bowl barrows that were chosen rather than the fancy varieties. Metal items were seldom placed with the burials, which were almost always cremations. Some cremations were placed in ceramic vessels and these were of varying size and style. Cremation cemeteries were often located around existing barrows, but some were placed in open ground on new sites. The burials often occurred singly, or in small groups, within barrows. Where larger groups survive, often from the cremation cemeteries, the total spread of graves can usually be seen to have occurred in discrete units or clusters. Analysis of these sites has shown that these clusters contain between ten and thirty burials, some in urns and some placed alone in small pits.

The most well known single urn cluster is that excavated by Miles within The Deverel Barrow, Milborne St Andrew barrow 14. At the level of the pre-barrow ground surface the excavators uncovered a series of large stones set in a semicircle (**24**). Sixteen upright cremation urns lay beneath the red non-local sandstone boulders of the stone setting while three more lay beneath isolated stones. Within the area defined by the semicircle were five cists containing unaccompanied cremations and four more cremations lying on the old ground surface. In addition, in the western part of the barrow, two small flint cairns covered three upright bucket urns and an inverted Collared Urn. The two largest stones did not cover burials and seem to form a pair defining the opening of the semicircle. There was no obvious patterning in the locations of fine decorated vessels, medium-sized everyday pots or large storage-type containers. However, the ordered layout of the stone horseshoe suggests that all the burials may have been interred in a fairly short space of time, all of them prior to the construction of the mound. The cremation cemeteries at Simons Ground, near Hampreston in Dorset, provide very clear examples of Middle Bronze Age burial grounds that were developed in and around small round barrows on the heath land (**colour plates 7 and 8**). Four barrows were fully excavated by David White, three of them had primary urned cremation burials, and all had further groups of cremations associated with them. These included clusters of burials located on the barrow mound or just outside the barrow ditches, usually of the south and south-east sides, and, in one case, an extensive linear cemetery running over a distance of 24m. In all cases the spreads of cremation burials could be broken down into clusters of 6 to 23 urn burials, and each cluster contained a mixture of vessel types. Many of the cremations could be analysed for age and sex and it was found that there was no correlation between age, sex and the type or size of urn. Furthermore, individuals of all sex and age groups

23 *The Deverel Barrow, Dorset, photographed by Leslie Grinsell.* (© Crown copyright. NMR)

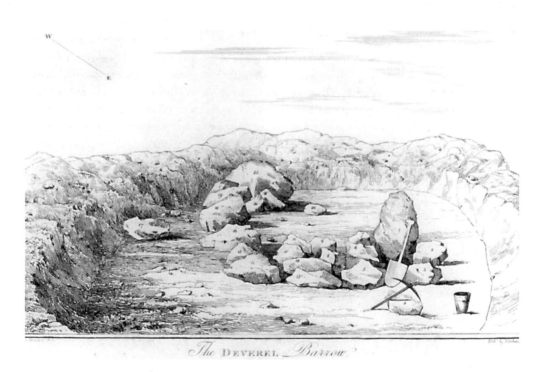

24 *The Deverel Barrow, Dorset: engraving by Miles, 1826*

were well distributed amongst all the clusters. Barrow Site B had three urn clusters and was the site that produced most in the way of other grave goods: flint flakes, a bronze pin and a spiral bronze finger ring.

Over southern Britain as a whole, most cemeteries can be broken down into discrete clusters, containing on average thirteen burials. On sites where the cremated remains have been analysed there is no correlation between age or sex determination and the style of containing vessels, and neither is there any discernible spatial patterning of age or sex groups. Burials of adults, juveniles and children of both sexes are found intermixed in all sites and clusters, and the distribution of finer pots or rare exotic items such as the fragments of metal ornaments amongst the clusters suggests that all clusters were roughly equal in status. Where exotic grave goods do occur they tend to be distributed one to each site or cluster. It seems likely therefore that the burial clusters represent the burial places for the members of separate family group or other social units of roughly equal size, each in use over a fairly limited period of time. These cemetery modules probably bore a direct relationship to the small hut groups that can be isolated on many Middle Bronze Age settlement sites. In several cases, small Middle Bronze Age barrows have been found sited adjacent to such occupation sites, and we shall be looking at one of these relationships in the next chapter.

Squares and circles

For the Iron Age, evidence for burials within barrows or outside them is extremely uncommon. The only area to have produced any number of barrows is eastern Yorkshire, and here they are mainly square in plan. Although a few square ditched barrows of Iron Age date are known in other parts of the country, and we shall be referring to a Dorset example in the next chapter, the major concentration of this novel type of monument lies on the Yorkshire Wolds. Unfortunately most of them are now ploughed completely flat. Many sites have been excavated and burials can be dated by the grave goods, such as brooches, beads, other ornaments and pottery, and by radiocarbon dates to the period *c*.400 BC to after 100 BC. The earliest barrows occurred singly or in small irregular groups. As time went on, the square barrow platforms became smaller, but the central pits were generally deeper. By *c*.100 BC the square ditches were closely clustered together in large cemeteries (**25**), and sometimes individual graves without mounds were squeezed into spaces between existing barrows. The barrows mainly occur on gentle slopes or run along the floors of shallow valleys and thus occupy lower sites than most of the Bronze Age round barrows found in the same area. Within cemeteries, the barrows appear to be arranged at random although some rows and alignments are apparent (*see* **25**, 1 and 3). However, where the barrows occurring in rows have been excavated, there has been no evidence for a simple linear development. Many of the cemeteries are closely related to contemporary trackways or linear earthworks (**26**), and some of the later groups seem to have been enclosed by ditches.

A small number of square barrows contained the remains of two-wheeled carts. This practice, and some of the types of ornaments found in the graves, can be matched amongst similar burials which were being interred during the same period in the Marne region of northern France. One such cart grave came from the very large area excavated at Garton Slack by Tom Brewster. Here a series of small groups of square barrows and Iron Age hut

25 *Square barrow cemeteries on the Yorkshire Wolds: 1. Grindale parish; 2. Kilham parish. The five barrows scattered to the south are probably earlier than the cemetery; 3. Rudston parish; 4. Kilham parish; 5. Grindale parish. Cemetery located along the floor of a shallow valley.* (© crown copyright, NMR)

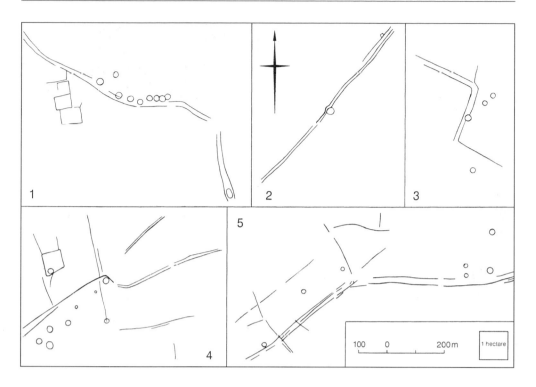

26 *Trackways and boundaries on the Yorkshire Wolds, aligned on or incorporating earlier Bronze Age round barrows.* (© Crown copyright. NMR)

concentrations were placed near the sites of some clusters of richly furnished Bronze Age round barrows, one of which lay over a Neolithic long barrow. The cart grave was situated in a relatively isolated position, but next to a round structure which may have acted as a mortuary house. The main surviving remains of the dismantled two-wheeled cart were the iron elements of the large wheels upon which the body of a sturdily built man, aged about 30, had been arranged. With him also were a whip and various harness fittings: two three-link bits in iron and various bronze rings and terrets, some of which were decorated with insets of imitation coral, and the whole elaborate deposit appeared to have been covered by the main body of the cart, turned upside down. Close relationships between barrows and settlement areas such as those at Garton Slack can be detected in other areas of the country and throughout prehistory. These are the sorts of relationships that will be the subject of the next chapter.

Notes

The key work by Fred Petersen is Petersen 1972; for Winterbourne St. Martin G46 see Gray and Prideaux 1905. The results of the excavation of Amesbury G71 are published in Christie 1967 and reconsidered in Barrett 1988. The monograph describing the excavation at Deeping St Nicholas is French 1994. Figures **11** and **12** are based on his figures 14, 18, 20 and 27.

The works on Neolithic round mounds and earthen long barrows are Kinnes 1979 and Kinnes 1992; for the Cotswold-Severn group see Darvill 1982; for bones as relics: Smith 1965 and Woodward 1993. Figure **16** is based on Lynch 1969, table 4 and Darvill 1982, table 4; figure **17** on Kinnes 1992, tables 2.6.1 and 2.6.2; and figure **18** on Kinnes 1992, pages 26 and 99-100.

References for the barrow excavations discussed in the chronological section of the chapter are as follows: Nutbane: Morgan 1959, Fussell's Lodge: Ashbee 1966, Willerby Wold: Manby 1963, West Kennet: Piggott 1962, Pant-y-Saer: Scott 1933 and Lynch 1969, Amesbury G51: Ashbee 1978, Shrewton G5e: Green and Rollo-Smith 1984, West Overton G6b: Smith and Simpson 1966, Barnack: Donaldson 1977, Figure **19** is based on his figure 11, Clandon: Drew and Piggott 1936, Lockington: Hughes in press, MBA burials: Ellison 1980, Deverel Barrow: Miles 1826, Simons Ground: White 1982, square barrows in Yorkshire: Dent 1982, and Stoertz 1997, Garton Slack: Brewster 1976.

3 Barrows as landscape monuments

Previous books on barrows, and the previous chapter of this one, have discussed the mounds as monuments related primarily to the rite of human burial. This has applied as much to the long barrows of the earlier Neolithic as the Early Bronze Age round barrows, the smaller round mounds of the Middle Bronze Age and the square-ditched monuments of the Iron Age period. As we saw in the last chapter, in many cases barrows were not the focus and sole resting place for the remains of one particular human body. Most were in fact raised over a series of burials, interred singly or in groups over varying periods of time, and such barrows often became the focus for cremation cemeteries which clustered around or between existing mounds. Various estimates of overall population and the total numbers of humans represented in contemporary barrows have indicated that in the Bronze Age not everybody came to be interred under, in or near to a barrow, and in the Neolithic the remains of even fewer members of the population ended up in a barrow deposit. Furthermore, some excavators have been puzzled to discover that their total or near total excavations of barrows have uncovered no human remains at all. This intriguing situation has occurred both in the case of long barrows such as Beckhampton Road and South Street, near Avebury (see p.31) or Thickthorn Down, Dorset, and round barrows, including Crig-a-mennis in Cornwall or two sites at Six Wells, Llantwit Major in south Wales. Mounds without primary burials have often been called 'cenotaph barrows'. What this means is that even when there are no burials, archaeologists have tended to assume that the mound was erected to commemorate the death of a particular person, but that the physical remains of that person were not available for burial — due to loss through drowning, death on a distant battlefield, or on a far-flung exploration or trading expedition. Thus, the excavated evidence has been forced into an existing preconceived idea, the premise that all barrows were built primarily as graves. In recent research, the topic of enquiry has been developed by some exciting discussions relating to the concept of memory. The results of several studies have reached the conclusion that there are two main categories of remembrance which are incorporated into the acts of building barrows in prehistory. The later concept involves short-term memory — the commemoration of a particular individual who is the member of a known family.

This type of memory exists within a family or other close-knit social group over a period of, say, three to four generations. Such commemoration of the dead relates more closely to our own modern system of human burial in graveyards or the ground of crematoria. However, it is thought that in the Neolithic the contents of the long barrows — regularly rearranged mixtures of the partial remains of selected individuals, some of which probably circulated within society as reverently venerated relics — relate more to a wider-reaching concept of memory. This concept would have centred on the idea of the human dead as a group of ancestors — a more abstract and all-embracing belief system that would have extended the thoughts of any human group into the far and distant past. These two contrasting systems are the two different concepts of temporality which have been defined by John Barrett. The earlier, belonging to the fourth and third millennia BC, the Neolithic period, 'evoked the idea of human existence as a process of *becoming*, a movement towards a future state which was described by reference to ancestors or gods', while the later concept developed in the second millennium, roughly equating to the Bronze Age period, when 'the weight of the past began to bear down upon the agent to fix an existence in *being*, a place and a moment where obligations and authority were situated in the directional flow of time. This may have involved a more complex definition of the person in terms of their status, and their genealogical position.' These ideas form part of one of the recent theoretical movements in prehistoric archaeology, namely the development of an archaeology of *agency*. This concentrates on the analysis of human actions, with the person being the 'agent'. It involves analysing the choice of actions or practices in terms of specialist or group knowledge, and the hidden meanings implied by those actions, rather than a more sterile interpretation involving the determination of function alone.

The aim of this chapter is to attempt a move away from the rather limited view of 'barrows as graves' towards a more generalised and holistic view which sees barrows of all periods as monuments, situated within the living natural and humanly-modified landscape of prehistoric Britain. Thus we move from a consideration of barrows as graves to the wider concept of barrows as artificial mounds. It is necessary to look at barrow mounds in relation to topography — the natural lie of the land, which has not altered since prehistoric times. Also to be considered is the probable contemporary vegetation, ranging from the natural wild wood variety to the ordered agricultural landscapes that had developed by Iron Age times. Thus we shall be involved in a process of unravelling the relationships between barrows and contemporary settlements, other barrows, fields and boundaries as well as with sites and monuments that survived, if only as earthworks, from earlier times. These relationships would have been both spatial and sensual. The spatial aspects, involving proximity and distance between sites and landscape features of different kinds, will be the subject of this chapter and the next, while in the final chapter we shall be looking as the more sensual aspects. Sensual perceptions relating to vision will be the main subject of enquiry, with studies of views in and out from barrows and monuments, sight lines, viewsheds and optical effects, but the importance of the other human senses will also be discussed.

Barrows in landscapes

Before moving on to a set of detailed case studies, some more general ground needs to be covered. We shall start by considering the earliest barrows, the long mounds of the Neolithic period. These mounds, which sometimes cover collections of partial skeletons, have been linked to ideas revolving around veneration of the ancestors, and their usually widespread but fairly even distributions across the landscape have led to interpretations hinging on the communal. Each barrow is held to have been a community monument, erected in a single farming territory. Applications of techniques of spatial analysis in the early 1970s suggested that some groups of Neolithic stone tombs and long barrows were located at central or peripheral points within discrete territories. Each block of land was thought to have belonged to a different group of farmers, and contained a 'fair' component of land with good farming potential. One famous example of such an analysis was Colin Renfrew's study of the Neolithic tombs on the island of Arran in Scotland. However, more recent research and fieldwork has shown that rather more monuments originally existed, and also that the cluster of tombs on the island was not typical of distributions on the mainland. Furthermore, archaeologists specialising in the Neolithic period have now realised that agriculture in the form of crop cultivation was rarely undertaken in the early Neolithic and did not become commonplace until the Early or Middle Bronze Age. In a detailed study of environmental evidence relating to early land use around Avebury, the late Bob Smith showed that the long barrows were fairly evenly spaced, probably in pastoral clearings in the forest. There was very little cereal cultivation, and the structure of the barrows used materials resulting from careful woodland management — coppice poles, willow withies and brushwood, the latter perhaps a by-product from hedge management, as well as turfs taken from pastures. Recent research by Chris Tilley and others is suggesting that long barrows were not related to particular settlements or temporary camps in any simple way. Instead they acted as key markers with the landscape. They were located on paths and trackways which showed to link camps and activity zones with various seasonally-exploited areas. They also would have led to production sites, such as quarries, or other places of ancient symbolic and ritual importance.

For the Early Bronze Age there is still, in many areas, very little direct evidence of permanent settlement, and it is thought that a predominantly mobile human existence continued until the Middle Bronze Age. It was only then that fields were laid out, and huts and enclosures of a more lasting nature came to be built. In some areas of Britain, round barrows are widely spread, in others they occur in regular clusters or in major concentrations around other, larger monuments. We shall be looking at examples of some of these later, but first there are some more general points to be considered. Firstly, it is fairly common to find, when barrow mounds are excavated, that the ancient soil buried beneath them contains quantities of apparently domestic material: flints, potsherds, animal bones and charcoal for instance. Sometimes this has been used as evidence for a pre-barrow settlement, the barrow having been deliberately erected over an old or recently abandoned or 'closed' habitation site. But structural evidence in the form of post holes, beam slots or pits is rare, and one interpretation favoured in recent discussions involves the idea of deliberate deposits of midden material. It is thought that specially selected portions of domestic debris, perhaps resulting from important feasts or seasonal celebrations, may have been brought from settlement areas and deposited intentionally as part of the funerary and barrow building activities. Further material of this kind is also sometimes found within the mound. The whole practice may have had its roots in the Neolithic, when some stone tombs were filled up with dark soil full of broken artefacts.

As well as preserving evidence of local agricultural practice, in the form of soils, pollen, charcoal, land snails and insects buried below the mounds, the structure of the mounds themselves may also inform us of contemporary farming processes. In upland areas the stony burial mound often incorporates stones cleared from areas that were being enclosed as small fields, although generally smaller stone mounds called clearance cairns often do not have any association with human burial rites. Another common material found in mounds is turf, either stacked as a primary core, or as a vertically sided major component of the barrow structure. Two recently investigated examples illustrate this trend. Turf and soil stacks were observed within several large bell and bowl barrows on the King Barrow Ridge, near Stonehenge, following treefall damage caused by the severe storms of 1987 and 1990. The decayed turf contained items of Neolithic pottery and flintwork similar to those found in the ploughsoil scatters along the King Barrow Ridge, suggesting that the turfs had been cut from the immediate vicinity of the barrows. Analysis of environmental material indicated that in the Neolithic period the grassland was open pasture with some shrubs, probably browsed or lightly grazed by animals. In the Early Bronze Age, immediately prior to construction of the barrows, the grass seems to have been grazed more intensively, and no settlement debris now occurred. The turf stacks in the barrows represent more turf than could have derived from the land covered by the mounds and ditches themselves. Indeed, for one of the barrows it was estimated that the area of turf used to build the stack was 1.2ha (3 acres), and this was thought to be very much a minimal estimate. Thus the six turf barrows which form the core of the New King Barrows cemetery might have used the turf from a minimum of 7.2ha (18 acres) of adjacent grassland. Does this major act, or acts, as the process may have taken place over several generations, represent a drastic change in land use? Alternatively, perhaps the incorporation of the turf from the whole ridge was a symbolic act, the claiming and subsequent sealing or 'hiding' of the whole land surface of an important sacred place, including all the items that had been deposited there during the previous two millennia. A group of nine round barrows at West Heath, Harting in West Sussex was excavated by Peter Drewett in the 1970s. The arrangement and nature of the cemetery, and the burials contained in some of them, will be considered in chapter 4. Here we are interested primarily in the turf stacks which occurred in eight out of the nine mounds. Soil analysis indicated that the barrows were built on degraded heathland soils. There was no evidence for much activity in the vicinity during the Neolithic period, so it is possible that the original soil was destroyed by roving Mesolithic bands before c.4000 BC. By the Early Bronze Age period there may have been some regeneration of hazel woodland but the vegetation was mainly grass and heather. As on the King Barrow Ridge, extensive areas of turf seem to have been stripped, but here there is no clear evidence that the area was an important or long-lived sacred place. However, the barrows are located on a distinct hillock overlooking the River Rother and such a place may have been imbued with symbolic importance by the local prehistoric people.

These last two examples provide indirect evidence for the continuance of a predominantly mobile way of life into the Early Bronze Age. Subsistence still centred on the gathering of wild plant materials, hunting and the herding of stock animals. However, in some areas of Britain, the results of detailed fieldwork are beginning to indicate that some settled agricultural settlements were already in existence prior to the Middle Bronze Age. One such area is the Peak District of Derbyshire where John Barnatt has been recording the remains of Neolithic and Bronze Age monuments, such as barrows and stone circles, which are closely related to contemporary Bronze Age settlement sites. On the eastern gritstone uplands, the barrows, stone cairns and small stone circles are all intimately connected with settlements. Each settlement seems to possess its own group of monuments and cairns arranged around it. However, they were not clustered next to the settlement itself, but placed separately within the agricultural landscape around the site. For instance, on Big Moor, the larger monuments such as stone circles and ring cairns are located in relatively private positions where the main agricultural and settlement areas could not be seen, while the barrows occur in positions on the fringes of the cultivated area. These barrow sites allow wider views, but good views towards the settlement do not seem to have been particularly selected. John Barnatt believes that many barrows in the Peak District were designed locally by small communities and that they looked out over the 'private' pastures of a single social unit. The important question of visibility between barrows and other types of site has been neatly introduced by this example — it is a major theme of modern research that will be considered fully in the last chapter.

By the Middle Bronze Age, at least in southern England, life was more settled, with small farming communities occupying well defined sites with a few timber huts, often enclosed and associated with small stock enclosures, pits for storage and groups of squarish 'Celtic' fields. One of the most famous of these farms is that on Itford Hill, East Sussex, excavated just after the Second World War. However, the reconstruction drawings of this farm which occur in many textbooks are incorrect. It was not a set of family establishments occupying contiguous enclosures, but a set of successive single farmsteads. Associated with the settlement site was a single round barrow, which, on excavation by the late Eric Holden, was shown to contain the cremation burials of a single family group, most of them contained in urns. Now, back in the early 1970s, I was lucky enough to have been invited to study this pottery, and we discovered that a distinctive sherd found on the settlement site derived from one of the very vessels that was used as a cremation urn in the cemetery barrow. This provided a unique link between the settlement and its adjacent barrow, and Richard Bradley was able to go on to establish a similar pattern of barrow/settlement links for many other sites of the Middle Bronze Age. Most prehistoric farming landscapes have not been excavated to provide information equivalent to that gained at Itford Hill. But it is still possible to make some considered observations concerning the relationships between barrows and other earthwork or cropmark features. On Grimstone Down in Dorset there is a complex pattern of surviving archaeological features, none of which have been excavated (**27**). A system of Celtic fields covers the hill; through it runs a hollowed track which runs east to a group of small and irregular enclosures which was probably the centre of settlement in Iron Age and Roman times. Next to this group there is a substantial dyke which appears to have been an early feature, possibly of later Bronze Age or Early Iron Age date. In amongst all these features there are seven round barrows, most of which probably originated in the Early Bronze Age. The barrows can be seen to have been incorporated into the farming landscape in various ways. The pair of two mounds, including the largest of all, 15a, lies within the open zone in front of the settlement enclosures and right at the end of the main track, while the second largest, 15d, was built into the bank of the track way. In fact the track seems to have been

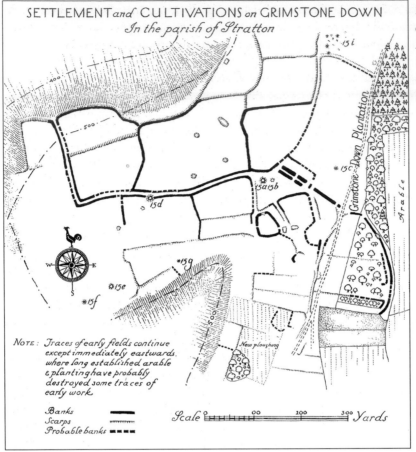

27 *Earthworks on Grimstone Down, Dorset. (© Crown copyright. NMR)*

laid out in direct relation to these barrows. The other smaller barrows lie at separate locations within different fields around the settlement, but they survived as mounds and were not flattened by cultivation.

During the Late Bronze Age and Iron Age periods in Britain, barrows were extremely uncommon. It is thought that most bodies may have been exposed to the elements or cast into water, whilst certain individuals, perhaps foreigners, criminals and suicides, were disposed of, or at least portions of them were, in pits on settlement sites or inside hill forts. By the Late Iron Age some communities in eastern England began to bury their dead in cremation cemeteries, but it was only in Yorkshire that barrows became at all common. And these barrows were very unusual. They were square in shape, sometimes contained rich grave goods including carts, and were constructed as part of very large cemeteries. Such barrows were described briefly in the last chapter, but how did these cemeteries relate to the contemporary settlement sites? From the extensively excavated sites at Garton Slack and Wetwang Slack we know that timber houses occurred in scattered unenclosed groups in places close to the cemeteries. Both farms and burials seem to have been sited close to linear boundaries, sink holes and seasonal chalk streams. The links to water may have been of symbolic as well as functional significance, and the distinction between square monuments for the dead and circular huts for the living may also have been both deliberate and symbolic. Interestingly, many of the associated Iron Age linear boundaries incorporate, or are aligned on, groups of earlier Bronze Age round barrows (**26**).

Wor Barrow and after: the Oakley Down cemetery

Wor Barrow, totally excavated by General Pitt Rivers towards the end of the nineteenth century, is probably the most famous of all the earthen Neolithic long barrows. It was reconstructed 'inside out', with an external bank, to provide an amphitheatre for community activities on the Pitt Rivers estate, and lies within view of the Oakley Down barrow cemetery on Cranborne Chase. The area is shown in figure **29**. Many of the barrows were excavated by Colt Hoare, and the resulting finds are housed at Devizes Museum. The plan in figure **28** does not include the entire Bronze Age cemetery — there are a few more excavated barrows and ring ditches just to the south — but the topographic setting of the barrows in relation to each other and to various monuments and features of later date are well demonstrated.

The barrows cluster around the head of a small bifurcating valley, now dry, which runs south-east to join the headwaters of the River Crane (**colour plate 9**). The earliest known monuments are Wor Barrow itself and the two adjacent barrows, numbered Handley 26 and 27 by Pitt Rivers. Following detailed study of the finds from the original excavations by the Cranborne Chase Project team, these barrows can be dated to the later Neolithic. They lie on the edge of the highest ridge overlooking the dry valley, just west of the modern track shown in the left-hand lower corner of figure **28**. The Early Bronze Age round barrows are not concentrated around these Neolithic barrows, rather they concentrate in three clusters: two groups of largely surviving barrows, one each side of the dry valley and a third, now ploughed out, across the head of the valley at the same altitude. Most of the extant barrows were excavated by Colt Hoare (nos. 100-113 and 118-122 on figure **28**), and one, no.115, much later in the 1940s; another in 1968 (**colour plate 10**). The cemetery includes various fancy barrows: two bells (nos. 102 and 121), five disc barrows (nos. 101, 103, 111-3) and a saucer (no. 114). Eleven barrows were found to contain one or more cremations and there were also three inhumations. There were ten rich 'Wessex' burials, including, amongst the grave goods, daggers, beads of amber, faience and shale, and two incense cups. At least one barrow was re-used for burial in the Middle Bronze Age and the only excavated barrow in the ploughed-out group (no. 115) contained three late Early Bronze Age biconical urns as well as an Early Bronze Age cremation burial. Continued use of at least some of the barrows in the cemetery during the Middle Bronze Age period may have been made by the builders of one or both of the Middle Bronze Age enclosures, the one known as 'Angle Ditch', situated immediately west of Wor Barrow, and the smaller rectangular one at 'a' on figure **28**. The Celtic field system outlined in figure **28** may have dated from this period; curved field banks around barrow a140 and a141 suggest that the field layout respected the sites of existing barrows. Barrow 123 transects another field lynchet, but which is uncertain. The field system was long-lived and was used probably by the inhabitants of adjacent Iron Age enclosures. Enclosure 36 has been tested by excavation. It was constructed in the Middle Iron Age over an unenclosed settlement of Early Iron Age date, and activity continued until the end of the

28 *Monuments and cropmarks on Oakley Down, Dorset.* (© Crown copyright. NMR)

29 *Oakley Down, Dorset, viewed from the south-west in 1970.* (© **Crown copyright. NMR**)

Roman period. The finds suggest that these farmers may have been of fairly high status, and their settlement was linked to the line of the Roman road by a trackway through the fields. A larger and more irregular cropmark enclosure surrounds a large portion of the hilltop, including the three Neolithic barrows. As we have seen already, the field system may have originally respected at least some of the round barrows at the head of the valley, but by the Iron Age and Roman periods they may have come under the plough. But the great bell and disc barrows, slightly further to the south, were reserved and therefore preserved in an area of permanent pasture. At least, that is, until the coming of the Romans, who erected a prestigiously substantial sector of their road, known as Ackling Dyke, right through the edge of the largest disc barrow.

In this little area of chalkland we can see a microcosm of prehistoric and later land use, affected and influenced by the placing of barrows. The Neolithic hilltop focus was avoided by the Early Bronze Age cemetery builders, although at least one of the Neolithic barrows may have had a Collared Urn inserted into it. In Wessex, this separation of Neolithic and Bronze Age barrows is relatively unusual, although it does occur elsewhere in the country. The round barrows are tightly clustered, in three groups, around the head of the valley. The Middle Bronze Age development of small enclosures and, probably, the first fields, overlooked the cemetery, and cremations were inserted into some of the barrows. As farming gradually intensified through the Iron Age and Roman periods, large enclosures were constructed and the fields began to encroach on the most northerly, and smallest, of the barrows. But the two main foci containing the large fancy barrows seem to have been respected. One was cut by the Roman road, but at least one other (no. 120) was re-used at an even later date, this time for the rich interment of an Anglo-Saxon woman.

Barrows in a valleyscape: the Bronze Age of Milton Keynes

In the early 1970s rescue archaeology units were springing up all over the country and, amongst the multi-county rural giants, there were others which related to the proposed major expansion of existing towns, notably Peterborough and Northampton, or villages such as Milton Keynes. This last type of unit has produced some of the most important prehistoric evidence that has been published over the last two decades. Along the upper reaches of the Great Ouse and Ousel valleys on the edge of the new town of Milton Keynes, a series of ring ditches were excavated, and the results brilliantly interpreted, by Stephen Green. Although, as we have seen, some groups of pottery and flints found underneath barrows may represent the remains of feasts or deliberate deposits of midden material, some long-lived scatters, such as those found under one of these Milton Keynes barrows, seem to indicate that the barrows were being built over settlement debris and therefore in the same zone as contemporary and previous occupation sites. The zone concerned is the low-lying valley floor from Milton Keynes north-east to Huntingdon, and it was shown that the barrows tended to cluster in small groups along the valley. In fact, in the length of valley studied, many of the ring ditches fell into at least nine groups which were spaced at intervals of approximately 10km (6 miles). As much of the land was already obscured from air photography by modern buildings or permanent pasture, it may be that the original spacing of the clusters was more like 5km (3 miles), giving an overall count of 18 groups or communities in the Upper and Middle Ouse.

Animal bones and environmental evidence from the excavated ring ditches suggested a pastoral economy with cattle herding and some hunting of wild animals. The four barrows contained the remains predominantly of women, babies and children. One could regard the Upper Ouse as a home base zone within a pattern of seasonal pastoral movements — the women and children having stayed at base, and been buried adjacent to the base camps, whilst the men may have been buried further away in areas of seasonal grazing. The overall pattern of barrow clustering and densities were compared with the more completely known distributions on Salisbury Plain, where the clustering phenomenon is common and where Andrew Fleming had suggested that the barrow builders were transhumant pastoralists.

However, how does the Milton Keynes pattern relate to the distributions of barrows and ring ditches known from some of the other major river valley systems? It is extremely puzzling to note that very little research into this question has taken place. Much energy has been expended on the crucially important recording and mapping of the remains, but discussions and interpretations of what the patterns may mean in terms of Bronze Age people are meagre indeed. One of the largest valley zones where extensive excavation and research has taken place is the upper Thames, especially the length between Lechlade, past Oxford, and down to the Goring Gap just above Reading. Most of this work has been carried out by the Oxford Archaeological Unit and recently some important summaries of the Neolithic and Bronze Age evidence have been presented, especially by Alistair Barclay. Below Oxford, complexes of Neolithic monuments, the most extensive of which is the one at Dorchester-on-Thames, occur at 5-10km (3-6 mile) intervals. Concentrations of ring ditches occur in at least ten large groups between Standlake and North Stoke, some of them in around the former Neolithic monument clusters and some close to the confluences of two rivers. These occur regularly at 5-10km (3-6 mile) intervals, and in between them there are smaller groups. However, the main clusters, several with more than 20 barrows or ring ditches, are rather larger than the Upper Ouse groups, and one of these, at Barrow Hills, Radley, will be discussed in the next chapter. Moving further north, it is interesting to compare the Upper Ouse results with the pattern of ring ditches along the Upper Severn as it runs from the mountains of Wales through rural Shropshire. Mike Watson has analysed the data from 25 years of aerial reconnaissance and has been able to demonstrate that the ring ditches also cluster in small groups. These are most common around Shrewsbury and along the lower reaches of the main tributary of the Severn, the River Tern. The groups are small in size, usually only two to four in number, but the largest contains twelve monuments. As for the Ouse valley, an interpretation involving a series of small communities has been advanced.

Where were these small communities living? The first systematic field walking projects, involving the plotting of archaeological finds found on the surface of ploughed fields, were undertaken by Peter Woodward in the Great Ouse valley during the early 1970s. In two areas near Bedford his team were able to demonstrate that flint tools and debris occurred in discrete clusters. These were interpreted as the ploughed remains of small settlement zones and one of the most interesting things about the scatters was that they occurred away from the riverine groups of ring ditches, slightly higher on the gravel terraces. The ring ditches themselves were located on land down by the river which could have been subject to flooding, at least in the winter months. However, much further down the Great Ouse basin, in the lower Welland valley north of Peterborough, where Francis Pryor and his team carried out extensive campaigns of field walking around 1980, a quite different pattern emerged. There were no clearly defined concentrations of Bronze Age flintwork, just a 'background noise' of medium density with occasional slight intensifications; these probably did not denote settlements. The team observed that the background spreads were similar to the random homogenous patterning of Roman, medieval and modern material in the topsoil and that, like them, they resulted from the practice of manuring of arable fields with dung and organic-rich midden material from animal enclosures and settlement areas. Therefore, the extensive flint scatter may reflect the area of Bronze Age arable, which on the higher gravel island at Maxey occurred around and amongst the monuments and ring ditches. From the flat gravel terraces of major river basins, we shall now move to the highland zone to look at surviving upstanding monuments in an area of much more varied local terrain.

Cairns and crags on Bodmin Moor

One of the areas of highland Britain that has been most intensively surveyed in recent decades is Bodmin Moor in Cornwall. Here an ambitious programme of work undertaken by the Cornwall Archaeological Unit and the Royal Commission resulted in the production of a model report in 1994. Thousands of burial cairns, clearance cairns and hut circles were recorded, together with almost 1000 hectares of fields and stone-walled enclosures. The huge variety of cairn types has been discussed already in chapter 1. Few sites have been excavated but it is likely that many of the monuments are of Bronze Age date. The huts are usually 5-7m in diameter. Some occur singly but most are grouped in small clusters, each comprising a large living hut and one or more ancillary structures for use as animal shelters, storage or craft production. In this way they resemble the small settlement units of the Middle Bronze Age in Wessex and Sussex, but in this more upland environment, many of the farmsteads may have been occupied only during the summer months. The doorways of the huts usually face south, and are sometimes emphasised by the use of large stone door jambs and porches. The hut groups are usually associated, or even integrated, with sets of conjoining enclosures and fields (**30**). Generally speaking, the settlement areas lie on sloping ground in-between the high ridges and summits, where natural rock formations and tors abound, and some more level plateau zones which are occupied by ceremonial monuments such as stone rows and stone circles.

The distribution of cairns, monuments and settlements is typified by the area of Craddock Moor located in the south-eastern sector of Bodmin Moor (**31**). One group of the settlement enclosures, those on the northern slope of Craddock Moor itself, is shown in the air photograph (**30**). This clearly demonstrates the general stoniness of the environment and the employment of stone in the construction of the many huts and boundary walls. In this area the highest point at Stowe's Pound is occupied by a prominent rock outcrop which includes the unusually shaped tor known as the Cheesewring. This hilltop enclosure may have originated in the Neolithic period. Small cairns and cairnfields lie fairly close to the zones of enclosures and huts on Craddock Moor and around Tregarrick Tor, and there is one kerbed boulder immediately north of the largest field system on Craddock Moor. However, most of the larger cairns occur between the settlements and Stowe's Pound in a fairly flat zone occupied by ceremonial monuments. Many of these large cairns occupy conspicuous locations and one of them, the famous Rillaton Barrow (**31**), contained a very rich Early Bronze Age burial within a peripheral stone cist. The main monuments are an isolated stone circle, embanked avenue and stone row on Craddock Moor, and, further to the east, a standing stone and row of three stone circles known as The Hurlers, which are aligned on the Rillaton Barrow and command a fine view of Stowe's Pound and the Cheesewring.

In the last few years a major campaign of very detailed survey and excavation has been mounted by a team from University College, London, concentrating on an area of settlements and monuments on Leskernick Hill in the northern part of Bodmin Moor.

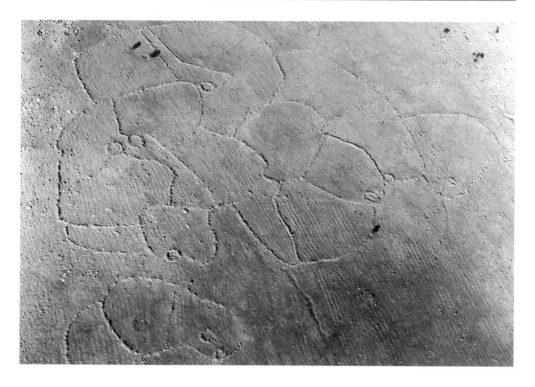

30 *Huts, enclosures and cairn on Craddock Moor, Cornwall. Viewed from the south-west in 1991.* (© Cornwall Archaeological Unit)

The area lies on a low hill, surrounded by rivers or bog and then by an almost complete circle of high ground which incorporates a series of hilltops. One of these is Brown Willy, the highest point on the Moor. The fields and enclosures fall into two main groups located on the south-west and south-east slopes of the hill, notably separate from a single large kerbed cairn which is sited, out of view, on the top of the hill. Amongst the fields and enclosures many stone huts are incorporated, and there are also four small cairns arranged along the southern margin of the enclosed area, plus one near the northern margin. To the south-east of the settlement area, arranged on a relatively flat zone of land, is a stone row running up to a large cairn at its western end. Either side of the cairn, and in line with it, there are also two stone circles. Views out from the south facing doorways of the huts would have encompassed this group of small but shapely monuments, together with the ceremonies and processions there enacted, whilst more distant views from the settlement would have encountered the ring of hilltops, most of which were surmounted by tors and large cairns of various forms.

All these patterns of localised small monuments and small cairns lying in opposition to the large hilltop cairns and the tors augmented by human agency are not dissimilar to the pattern observed by John Barnatt in the Peak District. Earlier we saw how the settlement areas on the eastern gritlands are associated with local cairns and small monuments, whilst the large stone circles and cairns lie on higher ground, in more isolated locations.

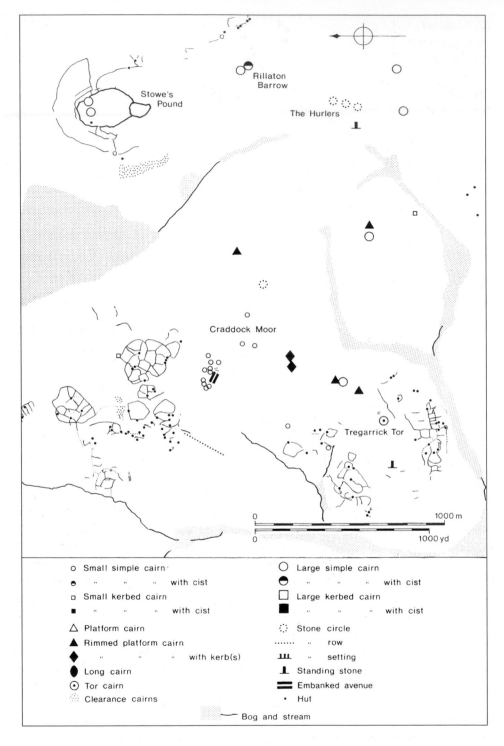

31 *Cairns, monuments and settlements in the Craddock Moor and Stowe's Pound area, Cornwall.* (© Crown copyright. NMR and © Cornwall Archaeological Unit)

32 *Long and round barrows on Rockbourne Down, Hampshire. sp: Spring Pond (© Crown copyright. NMR)*

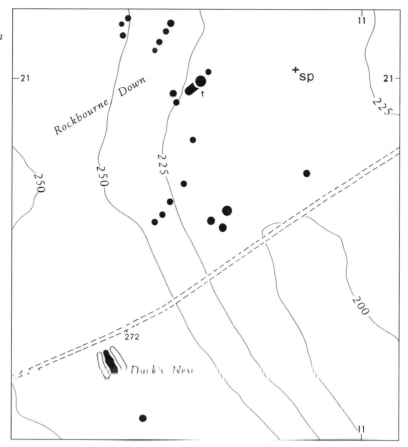

Rivers and watersheds

We have seen that the barrow cemetery on Oakley Down grew up around the head of a chalkland valley, and now we shall consider a Hampshire cemetery which was clustered not only at the head of a valley, but around a series of springs, which, at least in modern times, have fed a large pond (**32**). At Rockbourne, on high ground around the head of a stream which runs into the River Avon, there are no less than four Neolithic barrows, all of them aligned roughly north-west to south-east. Then, through the Early Bronze Age, a cemetery of round barrows was established around the Spring Pond. The barrows occur in short rows or clusters of between three to six, and one of the few excavated examples contained part of an urn with a flint arrowhead.

The largest barrow (**32**, left and **33**, right) appears to have been a disc barrow, which was later impinged upon by two subsequent bowl barrows immediately to the south-west. Many of the barrows survived as mounds when they were recorded by Grinsell in the 1930s, but now all of the round barrows are ploughed flat. Also visible on the air photograph (**33**) are the traces of a Celtic field system which seems to have the same alignment as a linear run of five barrows in the centre of the photograph, but they were laid out so that the barrows lay just outside the set of fields. These fields probably belonged to an Iron Age settlement a little further north which, in turn, integrated a row

33 *Round barrows on Rockbourne Down, viewed from the east.* (© Crown copyright. NMR)

of three small barrows into one of its enclosure banks. This settlement was later cut across by the ditch of a very large kite-shaped ditched enclosure that was built during the Roman period. This enclosure may have been intended for stock and it opened to the south, just next to the Spring Pond, which had presumably been an important water source for the local farmers throughout the prehistoric period. That the pond was also visited and venerated as a symbolic focus is highly likely.

The work of John Barnatt in the Peak District showed that barrows and cairnfields were associated with settlements in a local and intimate way. The barrows were sited slightly higher such that views across a small farm holding could be experienced but the overall patterns of distribution were on a relatively small scale. On the North York Moors, in an area of higher altitude and more extreme topography, a larger scale pattern has been detected. In the north-western sector of the moors, Bronze Age remains are exceptionally well preserved, and Don Spratt was able to reconstruct a system of land use and large scale territorial arrangements for the Early Bronze Age period. Whilst barrows containing Beakers and Food Vessels occur mainly in the same areas as Neolithic axes, in a zone skirting the edges of the high moors, those which produced Collared Urns occur also in the highest moorland areas, and, in particular, along the watersheds. As Food Vessels and Collared Urns were largely contemporary this dichotomy seemed to suggest a different function for the watershed barrows, which lie away from the traditionally settled areas on the periphery of the moors. Some of the watershed barrows contained richly furnished, often male burials placed in coffins, and Spratt felt that this might be a clue to social arrangements in the period. Maybe there

1 *Wayland's Smithy, Oxfordshire. The reconstructed façade in 1964. (© Crown copyright. NMR)*

2 *Bincombe barrow 31, Dorset. Half of the barrow has been ploughed almost away while the remaining portion survives on a road verge. (© Dorset Natural History and Archaeological Society)*

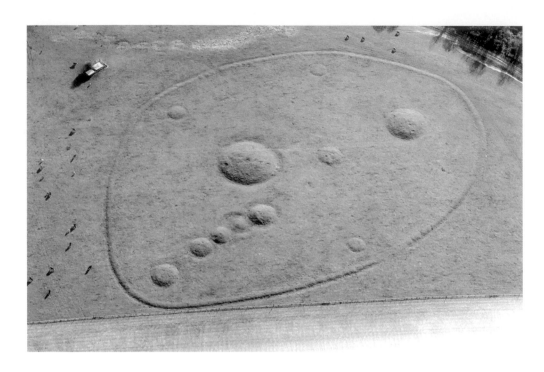

3 *The Winterbourne Stoke East barrow group.* (© Crown copyright. NMR)

4 *Belas Knap megalithic tomb, Gloucestershire: the false portal.* (Peter Leach)

5 *Early Bronze Age objects of gold, amber, shale and pottery found in the Clandon Barrow, Dorset.* (© Dorset Natural History and Archaeological Society)

6 *Early Bronze Age objects of gold, copper and pottery from the Lockington barrow, Leicestershire.* (G. Norrie and Birmingham University Field Archaeology Unit)

7 *Simon's Ground, Dorset, barrow F: the causewayed ring ditch viewed from the south-east.* (David White. © Dorset Natural History and Archaeological Society)

8 *Simon's Ground, Dorset: Middle Bronze Age cremation urn in the linear cemetery outside barrow F.* (David White. © Dorset Natural History and Archaeological Society)

9 Part of the Oakley Down barrow group, Dorset, located on a spur between two dry stream valleys. (© Francesca Radcliffe)

10 *Oakley Down barrow 100, 'rescue' excavated by the traditional quadrant method in 1968.* (David White. © Dorset Natural History and Archaeological Society)

11 *Row of barrows on the scarp edge at Bincombe Hill, Dorset.* (© Francesca Radcliffe)

12 *Two barrow cemeteries, Grinsell's Winterbourne Stoke East and West groups, are perched one either side of the narrow valley of the River Till.* (© Crown copyright. NMR)

13 *The Five Marys, Dorset: a row of barrows arranged along the top of a narrow ridge*
(© Francesca Radcliffe)

14 *Looking south down the Derwent valley from a barrow on Stanton Moor, Derbyshire.*
(Peter Woodward)

15 *The Snail Down barrow group, Wiltshire, viewed from the south-west.*
(© Crown copyright. NMR)

16 *The Poor Lot barrow group, Dorset, viewed from the south.* (© Francesca Radcliffe)

17 *Knowlton, Dorset: Church Henge, the Great Barrow and cropmarks.*
(© Crown copyright. NMR)

18 *Rudston, Yorkshire: the view west from the monolith.* (Peter Woodward)

19 *Rudston, Yorkshire: the view south from the monolith.* (Peter Woodward)

20 *Rudston, Yorkshire: view from a barrow near Rudston Beacon towards the church.* (Peter Woodward)

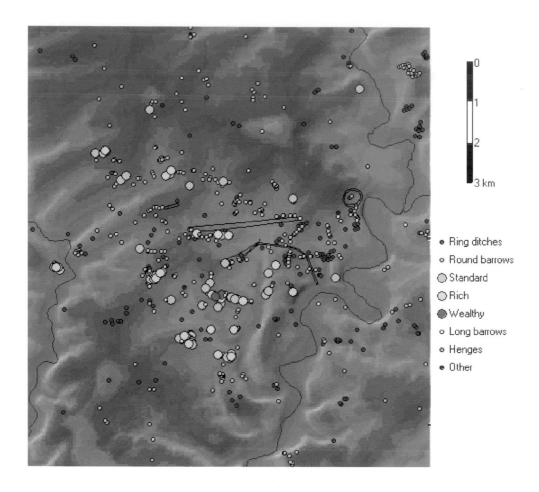

Legend:
- Ring ditches
- Round barrows
- Standard
- Rich
- Wealthy
- Long barrows
- Henges
- Other

0
1
2
3 km

21 *Three categories of Wessex graves: standard, rich and wealthy, in the Stonehenge region.*
(© Exon, Gaffney, Woodward and Yorston)

22 *Clandon Barrow, situated alone on the same prominent ridge as Maiden Castle.*
(© Francesca Radcliffe)

23 *Petre Ifan, Pembrokeshire: view of the stone chamber with the profile of Carn Ingli behind.*
(Peter Leach)

24 *Gwal y Filiast, Pembrokeshire: megalithic tomb situated in a valley. Chris Tilley has pointed out that this monument lies above, and in hearing of, a series of rapids on the River Taf.* (Peter Leach)

25 *Barrow and sink holes on Bronkham Hill, Dorset.* (© Francesca Radcliffe)

26 *Hambledon Hill, Dorset: the excavated long barrow lies towards the right of the photograph, just outside the cropmark of the causewayed enclosure, while the larger barrow is visible in the foreground, just left of the lateral rampart within the Iron Age hillfort.* (© Francesca Radcliffe)

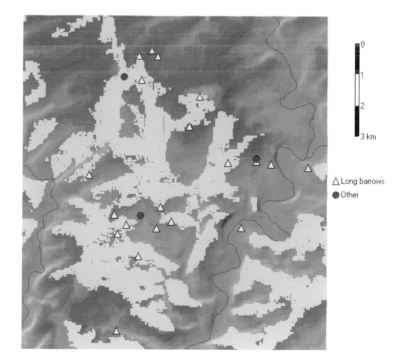

27 *Land and early Neolithic sites visible from the Knighton Down long barrow.* (© Exon, Gaffney, Woodward and Yorston)

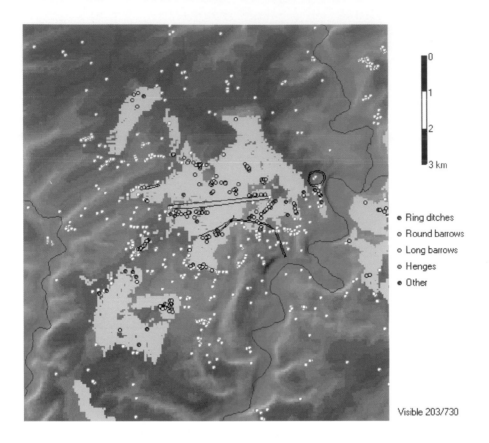

0
1
2
3 km

• Ring ditches
○ Round barrows
○ Long barrows
○ Henges
• Other

Visible 203/730

28 *Land and Neolithic to Early Bronze Age sites visible from the Stonehenge Avenue at the point where it crosses the King Barrow Ridge.* (© Exon, Gaffney, Woodward and Yorston)

29 *The Lanceborough King Barrow and associated cropmarks, with the ramparts of the Iron Age hillfort of Maiden Castle behind.* (© Dorset Natural History and Archaeological Society)

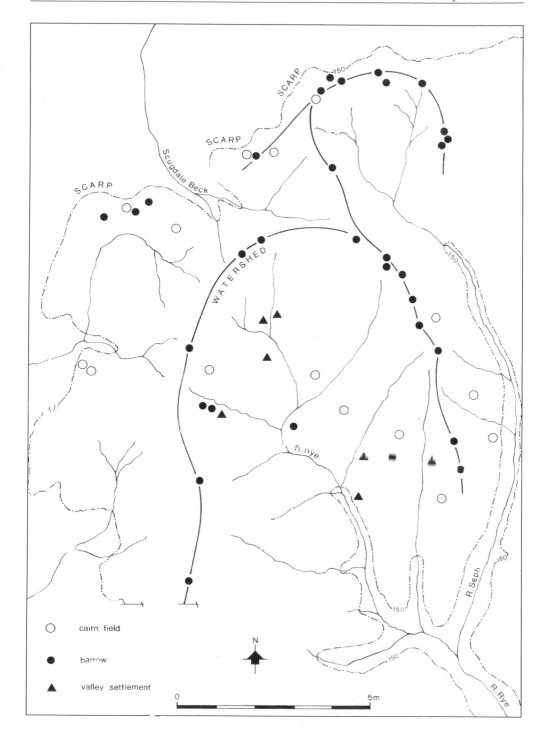

34 *Barrows, settlements and boundaries on the North York Moors.* (after Spratt)

was a group of high-ranking individuals who controlled large territories above the level of the local farms.

As well as the barrows, other surviving monument classes of probably Early Bronze Age origin are valley settlements in the higher reaches of the dales, and cairnfields (**34**). The cairnfields are usually associated with either stone walls or lynchets and seem to be the result of land clearance for fields. There were no permanent houses, but the existence of some lynchets indicates that the fields were for arable use as well as for stock. Often they were linked to the valleys below by deep hollow trackways. Spratt thought that seasonal use of such areas was made by large social groups who were predominantly pastoral but with permanent home bases on the periphery of the moors. The natural boundaries between such neighbouring groups were the major watersheds and these were now marked out and emphasised by rows of round barrows containing the bodies of territorial leaders contained in Collared Urns. The areas between the tributary streams in each catchment may then have been the territories of individual farming families, each with their own cairnfield. This overall pattern of land use probably continued into the Iron Age and, in terms of the modern township boundaries of the upper Ryedale area, it has in fact survived until the present day.

Farm and farmers on Cranborne Chase: South Lodge Camp and Barrow Pleck

In the Middle Bronze Age it can be demonstrated that settlement and burial became more intimately connected, both on the ground and, presumably, in the minds of the people occupying the sites. We have seen above that a pattern of small settlement enclosures containing pairs of huts were associated with adjacent cemeteries, some in small barrows freshly built for the purpose and some in and around existing round barrows of Early Bronze Age date. One of the most important sites of this kind studied in recent years has been South Lodge Camp, located in Cranborne Chase and roughly on the border between Wiltshire and Dorset, and the groups of barrows next to it which are called Barrow Pleck (**35**). Both sites were extensively excavated by General Pitt Rivers in the last decade of the nineteenth century and were re-examined in the 1970s by John Barrett and Richard Bradley as part of the Cranborne Chase Project. South Lodge Camp, famous for the finds of Middle Bronze Age metalwork and a complete Barrel Urn in its ditch filling made by Pitt Rivers was re-excavated by the twentieth-century team. Within the interior they discovered the postholes of two circular structures (**35**, A and B), a mound of burnt flint and associated scatters of pottery and flint. Re-examination of the barrows revealed that the mounds had been fully dealt with by the General but excavation of some zones of unexcavated ditch deposits, and the areas beyond the ditches, led to the discovery of several more cremation burials and parts of further urns. Thus we now know that Barrow 3 contained a minimum of eleven cremations, Barrow 2 had at least four and Barrow 4 one. No burials were recovered from Barrow 18. Most of the cremations from the modern excavation (those from the Pitt Rivers campaign were lost) were of adults of unknown sex, with only one child identified. Some were associated with portions or sherds from urns similar to those found in the enclosure. A few burials were centrally located in the mounds, some were peripheral, some were secondary deposits in the ditches and others were on or outside the south-facing ditch causeways.

*35 South Lodge
Camp and Barrow
Pleck, Wiltshire.
(after Barrett,
Bradley and Green)*

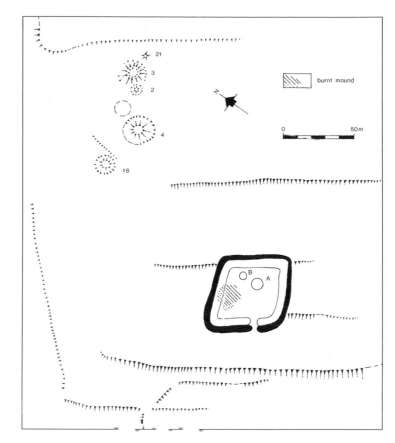

All this conforms very nicely to the pattern of single family enclosures related to small cremation cemeteries as discussed earlier in the chapter. However, the really interesting result of the modern excavation was the discovery that the sequence of events at both settlement and barrows was far more complicated than might have been imagined. Firstly, several of the barrows seem to have been restructured one or more times. Although there were some late Neolithic and Early Bronze Age sherds and flints present, it could not be proved that any of the Barrow Pleck barrows had originated in the Early Bronze Age; but it is possible that the largest, Barrow 4, had. The Celtic field system is also of several phases. The main lynchets pre-date the South Lodge enclosure and were probably associated with an unenclosed settlement. It seems that the burnt mound may have begun to accumulate at this time too. The enclosure ditch was dug to define a settlement area occupying two former fields, and took in most of the existing burnt mound. But the fields seem to have gone out of use at this time. What this means is that the Middle Bronze Age enclosure plus barrow and fields idea may be an oversimplification. Certainly at South Lodge, the pairing of sites may reflect a pattern that had already existed in the Early Bronze Age, and the fields may have related to that earlier pattern rather than to the main phase of Middle Bronze Age activity. As always, meticulous and extensive modern excavation throws up as many questions as answers.

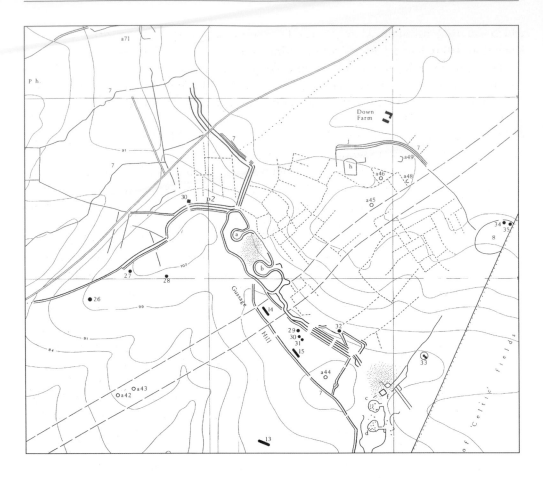

36 *Earthworks and cropmarks on Gussage Cow Down, Cranborne Chase, Dorset.*
(© Crown copyright. NMR)

From cursus to double banjos: Gussage Cow Down

The chunk of Dorset landscape shown in figure **36**, which is taken from the Royal Commission's *Bokerley Dyke* volume of 1990, is famous but little visited. The amazing complex of monuments, boundaries, enclosures and fields was illustrated by Colt Hoare in 1821 and by Charles Warne in 1872 (**37**). At those times, all the features survived as earthworks; indeed many of them still survived in the 1920s when a splendid air photograph of them was published by Crawford and Keiller. Sadly the complex is now almost entirely levelled by ploughing, and the features recorded in figure 36 only show as marks in the ripening cereal crops, but it was still possible for the Iron Age elements to be reassessed by Mark Corney within the Cranborne Chase Project. Figure **38** shows the south central sector of the study area, as it appeared in a near vertical air photograph of 1924. The area is a zone of chalkland with a series of distinct ridges and valleys running north-west to south-east. The summit of Gussage Hill overlooks the headwaters of the River Allen to the north-east and the Gussage Brook to the south-west. These streams, which now run only in the winter, join and run southwards past the henge monuments at Knowlton (**49**) to join the River Stour at Wimborne.

The earliest visible monuments are three long barrows; none have been excavated but they presumably are of earlier Neolithic date. Numbers 14 and 15 are ranged along the summit of Gussage Hill, whilst the longest one, number 13, occupies a spur to the south-west. Long barrow 13 is very prominently sited and is designed such that, at the time of the winter solstice, the sun sets directly over the barrow. This barrow subsequently became a focus along the route of the Dorset Cursus, and was totally flanked by the two widely-spaced banks and ditches of this monument which runs roughly from north-east to south-west in figure **36**. The Early Bronze Age round barrows, of which only one has been excavated in modern times, fall into three groups. Three of them, 26-8, are spaced along a spur overlooking the Gussage Brook, six (29-33 and a44, a disc barrow) look the other way, and seven more occupy more low-lying positions. The final barrow to mention is number 30. This is one of the few Iron Age square barrows known from southern England. The dating was confirmed by excavation in the 1960s but had possibly been robbed in antiquity. The plan in Colt Hoare's *Ancient Wiltshire* of 1821 and Warne's figure of 1872 (**37**) depicts two barrows in this location, situated either side of the entrance through the quadruple linear ditch system which occupies the north-west flank of the spur where the dispersed round barrows had previously been built. This quadruple ditch system forms one component of a remarkable array of multiple boundaries and two sets of twin funnel necked enclosures ('a' to 'd' on figure **36**) known as 'banjos'. A similar enclosure at nearby Gussage All Saints, excavated by Geoffrey Wainwright, had occupation phases that spanned the entire Iron Age and early Roman periods. The multiple ditch system is probably of Late Iron Age date, but the Celtic field system, which occurs north-east of the main boundary alignment, may have earlier origins. Enclosure 'h' has produced Early Iron Age pottery whilst 'a49' is of Middle Bronze Age date. Although Mark Corney has noted that the layout of the field system appears to have been influenced by the alignment of the ditches of the Dorset Cursus, little recent discussion of the potential relationship between the pattern of Neolithic and Bronze Age monuments and those of Iron Age and Roman date has been attempted. However, Colt Hoare was very well aware of the possible spatial implications, even thought the time depth of the sequence was not appreciated by him. He wrote: 'I hope I may not by considered as too fanciful, in attributing this long line of bank and ditch to the amusement of the Britons as a Cursus . . . ; or if my ideas on the subject be deemed too fanciful, let us suppose it to have been a grand avenue of approach to the British settlement; for certain it is, that these regular banks had some important communication with the works', ie. the Late Iron Age ditch systems.

The point is that the Cursus banks survived into the Iron Age and Roman periods and may well have been employed as a processional way within the Iron Age earthwork complex. Although the path of the Cursus is apparently blocked by the latest phase of the main earthwork boundary, it still heads straight for long barrow 14, a massive and stunningly sited monument that survives to the present day. The Iron Age landscape appears to be divided into a regulated enclosed agricultural zone onto which the entrances of the banjo enclosures divulge, and a more empty area to the south-west of the main boundary line. This empty area is occupied by the three long barrows and many of the

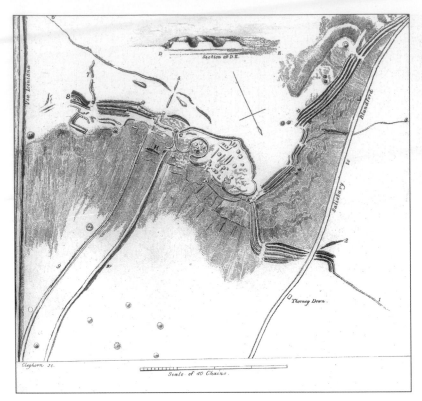

37 Engraving of earthworks on Gussage Cow Down from Warne's Ancient Dorset. (© Crown copyright. NMR)

round barrows. Perhaps these early barrows were viewed as ancestral monuments by the Iron Age communities. Certainly the main entrance to this zone was flanked by one, or perhaps two, Iron Age square barrows, and the focal long barrow, number 14, plus another long barrow and four round barrows occupy an otherwise empty triangular area enclosed by multiple ditches. It is part of this triangular enclosure that is shown in figure **38**. It can be suggested that this area on the top of Gussage Cow Down was of such sacred importance that the hilltop itself, and the barrows built upon it, retained their special identity throughout prehistory and probably into the Romano-British period.

Barrows in a gravelscape: Stanton Harcourt

The concentration of Neolithic and Early Bronze Age monuments that were constructed around the remarkable stone-set henge known as the Devil's Quoits, located a few miles west of Oxford near to the village of Stanton Harcourt, will be examined in detail in the next chapter (*see* **50**). However, it will prove useful to examine how the chunk of gravel landscape developed after the main period of barrow use had passed. The area concerned is a zone of gravel terrace occupying a huge loop formed by the courses of the River Thames and the Windrush. The henge and the associated distribution of Bronze Age ring ditches lie in the centre of the zone, whilst in the Early Iron Age there began a highly distinctive pattern of agricultural land use which lasted through the entire Iron Age and Roman periods. This pattern involved a band of arable land following the outer edge of the gravel terrace, with associated settlement areas,

38 Gussage Hill south, a near vertical view in 1924, with north-east to the top.
(© Crown copyright: Keiller Collection. NMR)

skirting a central area of probable pasture. At the Iron Age and Roman site of Gravelly
Guy, excavated by George Lambrick, it was possible to demonstrate that the linear
spread of pits lay in a boundary zone, with arable fields stretching down to the river on
the south. On the northern edge of the zone of pits was a row of small enclosures that
opened the other way, northwards onto the central gravel zone. Environmental evidence
suggested that this central zone was used as pasture and it may be that the pattern of an
inner pasture zone fringed by Iron Age settlements and then by arable fields may reflect
an organisation of the landscape which had already developed during the Bronze Age
period. It was in the central area of pasture that the barrows lay, and excavated evidence
indicates that some of them remained as upstanding monuments until at least the Late
Iron Age or Roman periods. The henge itself was also being ploughed in part by the
early to middle Roman period. The implication is that the henge and at least some of
the round barrows around it were still respected, and possibly venerated, throughout
the Iron Age period. Indeed, the largest, and focally placed, Early Bronze Age barrow
survived as a mound until the eighteenth century.

Notes

For barrows without burials see Ashbee et al 1979: Beckhampton Road, Drew and Piggott
1936: Thickthorn, Christie 1960: Crig-a-mennis, and Fox 1959: Six Wells. For ideas
concerning agency and memory: Barrett 1994 and Mizoguchi 1993; the quotation is from
Barrett 1994, page 136. The spatial patterning of tombs on Arran was analysed by Renfrew
(1973) and Hughes (1988); the Neolithic environment around Avebury by Smith 1984.

For the results from the tree throw holes on the King Barrows, see Cleal and Allen 1994, for the West Heath turf stacks, Drewett *et al* 1988. John Barnatt's work in the Peak District is summarised in Barnatt 1998. For Middle Bronze Age settlements, see Ellison 1981, for the barrow/settlement links, Bradley 1981. The east Yorkshire evidence is summarised in Parker Pearson 1999, page 132 and in Stoertz 1997.

The case studies are based on the following works, and the relevant barrow gazetteers published by Grinsell:

Wor Barrow and Oakley Down: RCHM 1990, Barrett et al 1991, and Brown et al 1995. Milton Keynes: Green 1973, Fleming 1971, Watson 1991 and Pryor et al 1985.

Bodmin Moor: Johnson and Rose 1994, Bender et al 1997 and Tilley 1998. § Rockbourne: RCHM 1979 and 1990.

North York Moors: Spratt 1982, figure **34** is based on his figures 43 and 44. South Lodge and Barrow Pleck: Barrett et al 1991, figure **35** is based on their figures 5.3 and 5.13.

Gussage Cow Down: RCHM 1991, White 1970 (square barrow) and Corney in Barrett et al 1990. The quotation is from Colt Hoare 1821, Vol. II, Part II, page 33. Stanton Harcourt: Barclay 1995, 113.

4   Anatomy of barrow cemeteries

Earlier in the book the complexity of barrows has frequently been emphasised. The neat division of barrow forms into bowl, bell, saucer and disc was found to be an oversimplification in lowland Britain, and the very large variations in cairn and mound formations encountered in the higher western and northern zones of the country were explored. When the internal structure of individual barrows of Neolithic or Bronze Age date was investigated, a pattern of great complexity was again revealed. Many mounds were built, extended and remodelled over several centuries, and burials of different types, representing single people or groups of varying size, were interred within the barrows in a multitude of ways. Therefore it will not be surprising to find that the spatial grouping of individual barrows into cemeteries presents an equally multi-faceted picture.

The traditional division of barrow cemeteries into two types, nucleated and linear, was considered in great detail by Andrew Fleming, who utilised the intricate and meticulous gazetteers of barrows in the southern English counties which had been published by Grinsell in the 1950s. Fleming defined nucleated and linear cemeteries as those where the distances between barrows are normally less than 100m, often considerably less, and also emphasised that individual cemeteries might display both characteristics. For instance, some linear cemeteries display a nucleated element (colour plate 11) For cemeteries where the distances between barrows varied from 100m and about 150m, Fleming preferred the descriptive term 'dispersed'. These dispersed cemeteries could be nucleated or linear in character. Finally, for zones containing many barrows but distributed mainly in ones and twos at of intervals of 200-400m, he coined the term 'area cemeteries'. Such area cemeteries can be large in extent, but are usually strongly defined by a surrounding zone devoid of barrows. Large nucleated barrow cemeteries tend to occur in particular areas such as the eastern sector of Salisbury Plain and the zone around Stonehenge, or Cranborne Chase, whilst other areas, such as the Marlborough Downs, have more widely spread small nucleated cemeteries, with only four to six barrows in each group. In contrast on the western side of Salisbury Plain and in central Dorset, the barrows are more evenly spread, with large area cemeteries.

Since the 1970s there has been very little research undertaken on the structure or location of barrow cemeteries. However, one element of more recent work is of particular relevance to our theme and that is the analysis of barrow siting in relation to altitude and aspect. One of the main conclusions that has been reached is that barrows are not concentrated in high and prominent ridge positions, but occur more commonly in valley locations, in deliberate conjunction with springs and streams. One example of such research is the consideration of the topographic locations of 2000 mounds — round cairns and barrows — in Wales, undertaken by Roese in the early 1980s. Only one third of the mounds analysed were found to occupy high locations on ridges and summits, or in passes. The vast majority lie in valleys, or in positions on lower valley slopes, spurs and knolls, or distinct ledges overlooking valleys. Where the mounds do occupy elevated highland locations, sites with wide-ranging all-round views are relatively infrequent, with most barrows occurring on ground sloping to the south, west or north-west. Some of the barrows which do command two way views are those which occupy positions within passes and these are often associated with stone circles or alignments as well. More recently, detailed consideration of the topographical setting of barrows and barrow cemeteries has also been applied to the contrasting area of south-east England. Here David Field has drawn attention to the small barrow cemeteries which lie fairly equally spaced along the low-lying minor ridge of the Folkestone Beds in the Greensand at the foot of the northern escarpment of the South Downs. These cemeteries are all situated close to rivers and the barrow clusters are aligned along the various small rivers concerned. However, many of the barrows face south away from the rivers and towards the South Downs, from where they would have been clearly visible. Some of these cemeteries also occur close to lakes and meres. The riverine distribution of Bronze Age barrows in also apparent within the Wessex chalkland where many notable barrow cemeteries are located at the heads of dry valleys or around the margins of deep combes. Examples include clusters of barrows around the heads and sides of the valleys of the Wylye, Avon, Till, Nine Mile River and the Kennet in Wiltshire and Berkshire (**colour plate 12**). Also such a pattern is common along the major river systems of the Midlands such as the Thames and the Ouse, or in the basin of the Upper Severn.

Combining the results and ideas from these two main lines of modern research — the analysis of the shape and size of cemeteries themselves, and the renewed realisation of the great importance of low-lying locations in watery places, it will be useful to explore a series of contrasting cemeteries in detail. But first, and to emphasise once more the considerable degree of complexity involved, the configurations of four Wiltshire groups will be examined (**39**). These plans have been prepared by English Heritage investigators as part of the results of a full survey of all the monuments located in the military training areas on Salisbury Plain. Each of the four displays very different spatial and topographic features. The Silk Hill cemetery could be described as a dispersed linear cemetery, but it actually comprises one major but uneven alignment of barrows running from a high point down the crest of a wide spur which juts east between two re-entrants of the Nine Mile River system. Within the main alignment there are two more nucleated sub groups, each of five barrows, and a centrally placed run of eight more closely spaced mounds, with a second separate row of four spaces a little further to the north. At Sling Camp, on the other side of the Nine Mile River, the large cemetery falls into two groups, one each side of a dry side valley. The barrows are fairly evenly spaced, but short alignments of three or four barrows are detectable within both groups. The famous cemetery on Snail Down, the plan of which will be considered in more detail below, lies at the head of a dry valley which runs eastwards down to the River Bourne, but all the barrows lie on the northern slope of the valley only. Finally, the group at Salisbury Plain Training Area Headquarters is in a ridged spur location and could perhaps be described best as a dispersed linear cemetery with nucleated elements

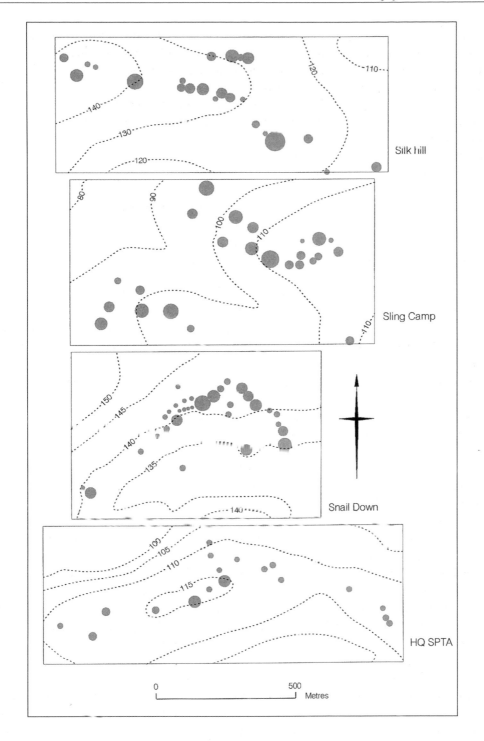

39 *Plans of round barrow cemeteries on Salisbury Plain.* (© Crown copyright. NMR)

Small nucleated cemeteries

A small nucleated cluster of round barrows was totally excavated at West Heath, near Harting in West Sussex between 1973 and 1980. Nine mounds in all were investigated by Peter Drewett prior to their total destruction within a commercial sand pit. The barrows were of varying size and complexity but all except one involved simple turf stack construction. The centrally placed barrow was the largest and appears to have been constructed first. Its first phase was marked by a large turf mound, about 20m in diameter, which was held in place by hurdling supported in a circle of stake holes. A ditch was dug two metres further out and the sand obtained was placed on the berm against the hurdling. A few centuries later, according to the radiocarbon dates, a second ditch was excavated outside the first and the mound was enlarged and thus refurbished. Around this focal barrow eight more were constructed. Five of them were simple, relatively small, ditchless turf stacks while one was slightly larger and surrounded by a single ditch. The final mound had two concentric ditches with an additional low external bank. The flat areas between the barrows were also investigated, but no further features were found to be present. A notable and extremely interesting aspect of the excavation results was that in only two of the mounds were any traces of human burials recovered. These were a cremation within an Early Bronze Age urn from an oval pit beneath the double ditched turf stack and a series of five urns, one of them associated with a cremation from a pit below a simple turf stack, sited about ten metres to the east. The simple stack also contained two more urned cremations that had been inserted into the mound during the process of its construction. Thus the large focal two-phased barrow may not have been a burial mound at all, but marked the site of repeated ceremonial activities which sometimes included funerary rites. Six of the other mounds also appear to have been constructed primarily for purposes other than burial.

The West Heath barrow cemetery is one of those sited on the Greensand ridge that was referred to earlier. It occupies a small low hill immediately overlooking the River Rother, which flows from west to east less than a kilometre north of the site. There are very fine views to the south, taking in wide vistas of the escarpment of the South Downs. Hillocks such as this would have been dramatic locations for the enactment of periodic ceremonies or festivals and would have provided a fitting resting place for the bodies of those who were eligible. Perhaps each group was built and used by a different segment of society, farmers and pastoralists who needed to keep a spiritual and practical eye on their far summer pasturelands on the South Downs.

A second small cluster of barrows, this time completely ploughed flat on a river floodplain, was totally excavated by Alison Taylor and Peter Woodward at Roxton in Bedfordshire. Here a group of five ring ditches lay immediately adjacent to the Great Ouse river (**40**). Through a process of meticulous excavation it was possible to show that the barrows had been of some architectural pretension. Only one was a simple bowl barrow, otherwise there were two saucer barrows and two of bell/disc type. Excavation between and around the ring ditches produced a further burial not surrounded by a ditch and flintwork of various dates. The three larger ring ditches lay in a straight line and were equidistant from each other. The other two, slightly smaller and now cut in part by the shifting course of the river, were markedly sub-circular (**40**). The first major activity on

40 *Ring ditches at Roxton, Bedfordshire, viewed from the north.* (© Crown copyright. NMR)

the site was the construction and use of post structures that were located underneath the sites of the three large barrows. The earliest burial seems to have been the skeleton of the mature man, along with some broken flint flakes, in an oval grave inside a semicircular setting of posts which may have supported an open-sided hut. This was located just west of the most westerly sub-circular barrow. This barrow, and the other one partly cut away by the present river course, were the first to be built and covered primary cremation burials accompanied by Collared Urns. One multiple burial of a woman and a child contained a bone bead, a bronze awl, freshly-knapped flint flakes and fragments from a pig's tusk. The other burial urn was with the cremation of a man plus child, and, although redeposited with a later burial, at least three perforated bone pendants of the kind that are known from several rich Early Bronze Age burials in Wessex. Whilst the more westerly of these two barrows had been constructed just next to the existing flat burial of the man inside the post-built hut, the other barrow appears to have been laid out from a central disturbance that was interpreted as a tree hole. Thus, to match the examples of stone cairns and barrows built around existing sacred earthfast boulders, or tors, in south-west Britain, here is an example of a barrow probably laid out and constructed around the trunk or stump of a large tree, which presumably held symbolic importance to the builders of the barrows. In the next main phase of cemetery development two sets of events occurred. Firstly the row of three large barrows was laid out over the former site of post structures that were now dismantled, and secondly, further burials were inserted into the two existing barrows. Interestingly, the large newly constructed barrows, although their structures were better preserved than the others at the time of excavation, produced no evidence of any Bronze Age burials at all. As at West Heath, the mounds seem to have been built for ceremonial purposes that did not include funerary deposits. But in the Middle Bronze Age period, according to the radiocarbon dates, new burials were added to the two sub-circular barrows. In one barrow, the Early Bronze Age central burial was dug out and into the resulting pit, which was enlarged to house a hearth, was deposited a new cremation of another man, along with fragments from the primary urn and the bone pendants described above. In the other barrow, a child cremation in the inverted base of an urn was placed under a small cairn of gravel stones in the silting of the existing barrow ditch. Associated with both these episodes of Middle Bronze Age burial there was evidence of contemporary flint-knapping; this again may have been associated with the funeral ceremonies and did not occur across the three large barrows immediately to the north-east. During the Iron Age the area was turned over to arable use and field boundaries, some of them visible in figure **40**, were laid out in a systematic manner. These fields were probably designed for seasonal use only and the barrows survived at least as low mounds into the Roman and Saxon periods, when further burials were interred on the sites of the Bronze Age mounds.

Linear cemeteries

Sometimes barrows occur in fairly straightforward lines, running along ridges or spurs, or on more level terrain. Such cemeteries may be aligned on the long axis of a Neolithic long barrow. This can be seen clearly within the famous cemetery at Winterbourne Stoke Crossroads (**41**) and, more simply, on Afton Down in the Isle of Wight (**42**). More commonly, they occur in more uneven linear patterns at intervals along major hill ridges. Examples include the various cemeteries along the South Dorset Ridgeway and some smaller runs of barrows next to the Ridgeway in Wiltshire (**47**). Others are more isolated. At Chaldon Herring in Dorset the linear run of eight barrows known as the Five Marys are closely spaced on a prominent ridge of chalk just inland from the main chalk downs by the coast (**colour plate 13**). The line includes three bell barrows and one pond barrow. Two of the mounds were dug into before 1866. One urn survives in the county museum, but the main burials found were associated with antlers. This may imply that at least two of the monuments began as Neolithic round mounds. The ridge commands fine views south into a hidden dry valley, and to the north far across the heathlands of central Dorset.

In the vicinity of Priddy, situated on the high ridge of the Mendip Hills in north Somerset, there are several important groups of barrows. Two of the main cemeteries are distinctly linear in nature and occupy the crest and south-facing slope of one of the highest hills of Mendip. From the cemeteries there is a view northwards across the impressive alignment of four henge monuments known as the Priddy Circles and eastwards down into a high level marshy valley. Among the Priddy Nine Barrows, at least three barrows appear to have been opened, but records exist in only one case. The nearby cemetery on Ashen Hill is another impressive linear group, although the alignment veers slightly to the south at its eastern end (**43**). The eight mounds are all bowl barrows, and are set in close conjunction with each other. All were investigated by the Reverend John Skinner of Camerton in 1815, and the fourth mound from the west (the right hand side of figure **43**), was further excavated by Balch in the 1890s. All the barrows produced one or more

41 *The Winterbourne Stoke Crossroads group, Wiltshire, viewed from the south-west in 1995.* **(© Crown copyright. NMR)**

42 *Long and round barrows on Afton Down, Freshwater, Isle of Wight.* **(© Crown copyright. NMR)**

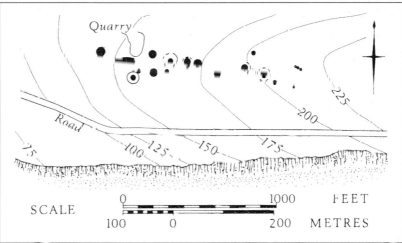

cremations, sometimes contained in Early Bronze Age urns which were covered with stone slabs. Three of the barrows yielded burials accompanied by bronze daggers, one of them in a wooden sheath, and one of these was a very rich burial which also included beads and other objects of amber, and possibly of faience, and a miniature incense cup. The isolated pair of barrows located south of the main cemetery, visible at the top of the air photograph (**43**) have particularly high mounds. The larger mound, known as Great Barrow or North Hill Tump shows evidence of having been opened but there is no record of whatever burials or riches it might have contained.

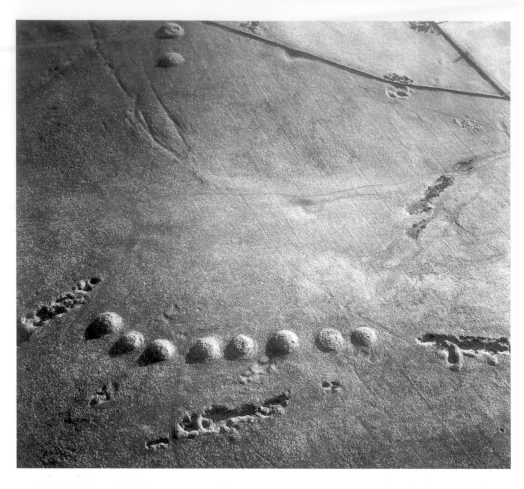

43 *Barrows on Ashen Hill, Somerset, viewed from the north in 1979.* (© Crown copyright. NMR)

Dispersed cemeteries

Groups of barrows which form particular clusters, but where the mounds within them are loosely spread over a relatively wide area, are common, especially in the highland areas of Britain. To illustrate this phenomenon we shall look at two dispersed groups of very different character: one a dispersed collection of Bronze Age monuments situated around the head of a valley in north Wales, but firstly the major group located on Stanton Moor in the Peak District of Derbyshire. In the last chapter the intimate and localised spatial correlations between small cairns, some larger monuments and contemporary Bronze Age settlements in the Peak District were discussed. However, there are also a few examples of larger areas set aside for funerary and ritual use. One was the zone around the substantial henge monument of Arbor Low, but probably the most extensive is the spread of monuments along the edge of Stanton Moor, on the western flank of the Derwent valley. This dispersed cemetery is particularly well known because many of the cairns were excavated by a local family, the Heathcotes, in the early part of the twentieth century, and the collection of urns and other grave goods that they recovered are housed in Sheffield

City Museum. The distribution of the different monuments on the moor has been studied by John Barnatt. Ranged along the centre of the heathland that has survived quarrying there is a widely spaced row, running roughly north to south, of larger monuments including several ring cairns, larger round barrows and, towards the north end, a stone circle known as the Nine Ladies. Arranged on either side of this axis there are many other mounds, mainly small cairns some of which are distinctly rectangular in shape, and some of which are surrounded by stone kerbs. Occasionally the small cairns are closely grouped in nuclear clusters or short rows, but most of them are irregularly distributed. Of the forty or so monuments excavated by the Heathcotes, just over half were found to contain grave goods, usually in the form of Early Bronze Age urns. Also, a chance discovery near the south end of the moor has led to the investigation of a small area of graves which were not covered by mounds, and it may be that many more such groups of flat graves may exist in and amongst the upstanding monuments. The reasons lying behind the choice of this particular zone of moorland for such a concentration of monuments will have been complex, but one of the factors may have been the existence of a stunning view which, below a very steep and immediate scarp, extends many miles down the valley of the River Derwent (**colour plate 14**).

A more localised group of dispersed barrows and monuments is the set of monuments in the Brenig valley, north Wales. Here, in the central moorland of Denbighshire known as Mynydd Hiraethog, Frances Lynch and her team excavated a wide range of circular Bronze Age mounds and monuments, prior to the construction of a new reservoir, in the early 1970s. The monuments were ranged around the sloping sides of the valleys of the headwaters and one sidestream of the River Brenig (**44**). Altogether eleven circular monuments were totally excavated and many were dated by the radiocarbon method. Five different categories of structure were encountered: large burial mound, small stone cairn, ring cairn, platform cairn and kerb cairn, and these will be described in turn. The four large burial mounds ranged in size from 16-24m across and were constructed of turf with a pale grey-yellow capping of clay above a series of circular layouts of timber stakes. Mound 40 (*see* **44**) lay over four stake circles. The monument was probably constructed in stages and the final mound was edged by a continuous wooden palisade. Under the centre were the remains of a timber rectangular mortuary structure. Although any original burial had been robbed out, fragments from the cremation of an elderly person remained. Mound 41 incorporated two stake circles which had supported hurdling, but a central burial pit had been robbed, only one fragment of unburnt human bone remaining. The mound succeeded a slightly larger free-standing stake circle or fence which had enclosed the hillock upon which the mound was sited. The only mound with a ditch was monument 42. This had one stake circle built prior to the mound and another which held revetment for the mound itself. There was a rectangular post structure at the centre but any burials had been robbed out. The most complex large burial mound was monument 45, which had three stake circles and an outer dry-stone wall with occasional upright stones, all pre-dating the mound. Later a larger irregular stake circle was added and the final mound was supported by an outer timber palisade which encompassed a small standing stone, 0.75m high. There were seven cremation burials, the first of which was interred in a central pit, possibly with an urn which had been extracted from the mound

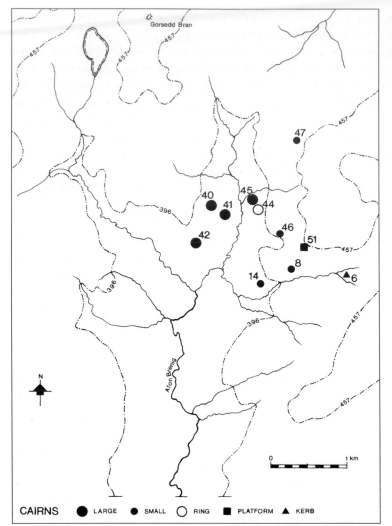

44 *Cairn cemetery in the Brenig valley, Denbighshire.* (after Lynch, with additions)

CAIRNS ● LARGE ● SMALL ○ RING ■ PLATFORM ▲ KERB

in 1850. Adjacent to the stone wall and widely-spaced there were further and later cremations of an adult, possibly female, a mature man, a young, probably male, adult, and small deposits from two other individuals. With only one of these burials, the younger man, there was an Early Bronze Age urn. The final burial was the cremation of a baby, less than six months in age, found inside a small plain urn, placed in the outermost palisade trench.

The four smaller cairns consisted of heaps of stone, 8-12m across (**44**). Cairn 8 occupied a natural rocky knoll and covered a cremation contained in a rock-cut grave. Two more, numbers 14 and 46, had been disturbed in the earlier part of the twentieth century. Two central pits under cairn 46 were empty but the cremation of a young child was found in a small stone box on the south side. Cairn 14 was also found to have one cremation burial, probably an adult, surviving. The fourth small cairn, 47, was found to contain neither burials nor grave goods. The stone mound was an enhancement of a natural promontory.

At the head of the eastern side stream lies the kerb cairn, number 6. This is situated close to the stream and near to a very large glacial erratic rock called Maen Cleddau. The kerb of large boulders, only 5m across, covered the remains of a circular timber structure with a hearth. There was a cremation at the centre of the cairn, and a further hearth just outside the kerb. On a prominent spur just to the north, at a point where all the monuments within the cemetery are clearly visible, lies the large platform cairn, 51. In the first phase this consisted of a broad and flat ring of stones with kerbs inside and outside and an open central area. Underneath the stone ring was a double burial, the cremated remains of two adults, together with an urn and a small bone terminal from the handle of a dagger. Within the central area was a deep post hole which may have held a ceremonial pole, perhaps carved, and near the edge of the circle was a child cremation. Not very much later the central area was filled with stones to produce a large level platform, with a marked concentration of shiny, white pieces of quartz at the very centre. Finally a small semi-circular cairn was added to the outer edge of the platform. This also incorporated much quartz and under it was a crushed urn containing a deposition of charcoal, but no burial. The depositing of charcoal, often in pits, was also the main activity at the most long-lived monument of the group, the ring cairn 44. This was a stone built ring, 2m wide, with an external free-standing timber circle. At a later stage sloping clay banks were added to both margins of the stone ring. Various pits were found, mainly around the edges of the central area and finally an extra semicircular cairn was added at the north-west. At first the pits contained charcoal only, but in the later stages of use, a series of burials were inserted. These included a cremation at the centre, and a complicated deposit in a pit on the north-east side. This contained the cremated remains of an adult and a child, each contained in an urn. With the child burial there was also a tiny accessory pot, a burnt flint knife and two pottery objects which may have been amulets.

From the structural sequences in the various mounds and a wide series of radiocarbon dates a broad idea of the development of the cemetery through time could be worked out. The ground surfaces preserved beneath the mounds and the turfs used to build them contained flint tools. Those of Mesolithic date concentrated only in the vicinity of monuments 44 and 45 and this may indicate that this particular spot was frequented from very early times. The earliest mound by far, on the basis of the radiocarbon dates, was the small cairn 47. This may have been built in the late Neolithic period but contained no burial. The excavator argued that this mound might have been an ancient territorial marker. From it distant barrows on the surrounding hilltops can be seen, and it forms the apex of the cemetery barrows below. It seems that the major monuments at Brenig were set out so that a clear view of mound 47 could be achieved. The main sequence of activity spanned at least four centuries, with the ring cairn (44) and two or even three of the large mounds being constructed first. The platform cairn (51) and large mound 40 were built next, whilst the ring cairn was still being modified. Finally, as the phase of human burial at the ring cairn was entered, the large mound 45 was re-used and the kerb cairn (6) may have been built.

The establishment of this dated sequence is very important because it shows that this dispersed valley cemetery did not develop in a simple progression, mound by mound. Instead there seems to have been a long and changing history of ceremonial activity centred on the ring cairn, with other burial mounds and monuments being constructed, used intermittently, and re-used over varying periods of time. The funerals and acts of interment appear to have occurred only occasionally and cannot represent the burials of complete communities or even the leaders or all the members of a particular section of the local populations. At Brenig ceremony seem to have been of greater significance than burial. The monuments were carefully sited in relation to the early mound 47, and all of them were visible from the platform cairn. The cemetery did not grow organically but was developed in a subtle and intentional manner according to an initial concept of some sophistication. Happily, the detailed plans for the reservoir altered; the excavated monuments survive above water level and an archaeological trail has been laid out around the north-east margin of the lake.

The Lambourn Seven Barrows, a cemetery which comprises many more than seven mounds, lies nestled in the remote chalk downland of west Berkshire. The barrows lie in the head of a twisting stream valley (**45**). In general terms this rather dispersed group lies around the top of the valley in a similar way to the monuments at Brenig, but the whole arrangement is on a smaller scale, and the central zone of the cemetery has become more infilled. Indeed, this central sector displays a layout incorporating two roughly parallel rows of mounds similar to those found in the cemeteries, which are to be discussed in the next section of this chapter. In wet winters, the seasonal stream or winterbourne rises at a point near the south margin of the plan, but it may be that in the Neolithic period, when the long barrow was first constructed, that the stream sprang at the very head of the valley, just below the site of the long barrow itself. Many of the barrows were excavated, in a surprisingly advanced and modern manner, by Edwin Martin Atkins between 1850 and 1858. Many of the finds went to the British Museum but it was not possible to tie in the grave groups to particular barrows until the 1950s. It was then that a set of letters written by Martin Atkins, together with a plan of the cemetery, were found in the Bodleian Library in Oxford and, using these and notes and drawings housed in the Ashmolean Museum, a piece of brilliant detective work by Humphrey Case led to a full decipherment of the excavation record.

The earliest known barrow is the long barrow, excavated at the time of Martin Atkins' investigations, and again in 1964 by John Wymer. Various sets of human bones were found, and Neolithic and Beaker pottery was found in the ditch filling. The earliest dateable burials in the round barrows were associated with Beakers in two very small mounds near the southern limit of the cemetery (*see* **45**). Burials of Early Bronze Age date included Collared Urns in the disc barrow east of the long barrow and in the southernmost mound of the eastern barrow row, while richer Early Bronze Age grave groups were found in a bell barrow close to the Beaker mounds and in the round mound, probably originally a bell, which lies nearest to the long barrow. This round barrow later became the site for an extensive cremation cemetery of the Middle Bronze Age period, and fragments of urns of this date from the long barrow ditch may have come from other burials inserted into its mound or upper ditch fillings. Several other barrows produced charcoal only or various animal remains. No clear pattern of linear cemetery development through time can be deduced from this evidence. As at Brenig, it may be that key points throughout the cemetery area were defined at the outset, some of

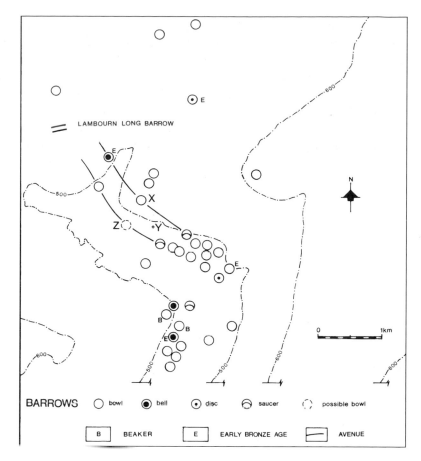

45 *Lambourn Seven Barrows, Berkshire.* (after Case and Wymer, with additions)

LAMBOURN LONG BARROW

BARROWS   ◯ bowl   ◉ bell   ⊙ disc   ⊖ saucer   ⟨⟩ possible bowl

| B | BEAKER | | E | EARLY BRONZE AGE | | | AVENUE |

them becoming the foci for later constructional developments of varying kinds. The more nucleated portion of the cemetery falls into two parts — the double row on the eastern side of the valley, and a more disparate group on the western side. The western group includes two fine bell barrows and several small mounds, some of which produced the Beaker burials, while the double row is mainly made up of bowls with a disc barrow at the south end and two saucer barrows at the upper end. The two rows diverge to the north-west, apparently defining a processional way which leads towards the long barrow at the head of the valley. However, the long barrow is not visible from the area of the close-set rows because the profile of a low spur intervenes. The barrow which sits on this spur (at X on figure **45**) is visible from all points, and walking up the line of the suggested avenue the long barrow first comes into sight at the point Y. The upper part of the route is defined by large but more widely spaced barrows, including a possible mound at Z which has not previously been recorded.

Row cemeteries

Many larger barrow cemeteries include a series of separate linear elements with differing alignments. Rather than including these in the category of linear cemeteries it seems useful to consider them in their own right. Therefore, using a term used more often in

85

the description of flat grave cemeteries, particularly those of the Christian period, a class of row cemeteries can be defined. One of the most extraordinary cemeteries which is dominated by several distinct rows of barrows is that at Poor Lot (**colour plate 16**). This occupies three different parishes in west Dorset and, like the Lambourn Seven Barrows, lies near the head of a major river valley system. As none of the barrows have any records of excavation in the nineteenth or twentieth centuries, possible sequences of cemetery growth cannot be deduced from dateable grave goods or absolute dates determined by the radiocarbon method. However, the internal spatial structure of the cemetery is clear, if extremely unusual. There is an especially high occurrence of fancy barrows within the cemetery and the inclusion of four or five pond barrows is particularly remarkable (**46**). Most of the barrows lie on the southern slope of the valley of the South Winterborne, or on the valley floor itself. Sited on a slight spur which extends into the valley from the South Dorset Ridgeway, which rises sharply to the south, are two separate rows of barrows, each on a different alignment. Across the eastern end of each row there is a much shorter row of smaller barrows arranged at right angles to the major row. The sequences of barrow types in the major rows, starting from the east end, both begin with a very large bell barrow followed by a substantial disc barrow. Running west from these the northern row has six bowls whilst the southern sequence runs: pond, bell, disc and bowl. The shorter perpendicular rows running across beyond the major eastern bell barrows both contain runs of small bowl barrows, but the northern one also includes a small pond barrow, a disc and two small bells. Halfway between the two major rows is a small cluster of two more possible pond barrows and a bell (Kingston Russell 7m-7o).

The two main rows each with a massive bell barrow at the east end and the row of smaller barrows across the ends almost seem to replicate the form of Neolithic long barrows, with a higher 'business' end and flanking facades. Both rows are aligned and focused on the very large pond barrow South Winterborne Abbas 30, which lies in the very bottom of the valley. In between there are a large bell barrow (28) and a double bell (26/27), whilst on the flanking slopes there are single disc barrows to the north (23) and south-east (31). From the spur where the two major rows are sited, all other barrows in the group are visible as well as the two long barrows (Kingston Russell 6d and 6i) and the South Dorset Ridgeway to the south, and the Martin Down bank barrow, which lies 1.5km to the west. Immediately north of that bank barrow, and in the very head of the dry valley of the Winterbourne is an isolated standing stone (*see* **71**), whilst another monolith, the Broad Stone, is situated a little way down the valley floor from the large focal pond barrow of the Poor Lot cemetery. This stone now lies by the roadside, but it was standing in the eighteenth century, and next to it is the site of yet another pond barrow.

Pond barrows are a very rare type. Few have been excavated, but that on Sheep Down in the neighbouring parish of Winterbourne Steepleton, investigated by Richard Atkinson, was found to enclose a circular area peppered with small pits. About one third of these contained cremation burials, some of them in urns, or token fragments of bone, but most contained earth only. Monuments such as these may have been the foci for repeated ceremonies rather than for formal burial and in this respect might recall the ring cairn that formed the long-lived focus of the barrow cemetery in the Brenig valley discussed above. At Poor Lot there are two very large pond barrows on the valley floor, the upper forming

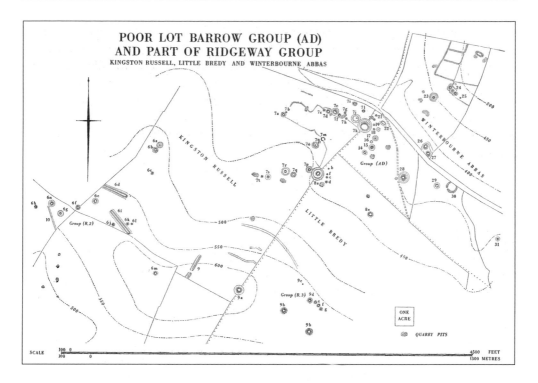

46 *The Poor Lot barrow group, with parts of Ridgeway Groups R.2 and R.3, Dorset.*
(© Crown copyright. NMR)

the visual focus for the two major barrow rows, each of which in turn includes a smaller pond barrow. The complex layout of the barrows of varying form and size in the Poor Lot group lies in direct contrast to two of the standard South Dorset Ridgeway barrow cemeteries, which are also shown in figure **46**. Both consist entirely of bowl barrows, and they are arranged in a loose dispersed cluster (R.2 amongst the Kingston Russell long barrows), and a short line with two outliers on the ridge (Group R.3).

Another row cemetery that appears to focus on a single pond barrow is located at Snail Down in the south-eastern part of Salisbury Plain. This complex and impressive cemetery occupies the northern slope of the head of a broad and shallow dry valley in the two parishes of Collingbourne Ducis and Collingbourne Kingston (**39**). Prior to the Second World War this was one of the best preserved barrow cemeteries in Wessex, but since then it has been much damaged by tank tracks. As the modern excavators noted, the barrows unfortunately provided an 'alluring series of switchbacks'. This damage, now halted by the military, is only too clear on the air photograph (**colour plate 15**). The cemetery possesses an unusual layout that comprises two sides of a triangle with its apex to the north. It overlies an extensive area of Beaker settlement and was, in the later Bronze Age, enclosed within a reserved area defined by a series of linear banks and ditches. The cemetery was investigated by Colt Hoare who dug into twenty-four of the barrows. Cremation burials were discovered in many of them and four mounds produced rich groups of Early Bronze Age grave goods. These included a fine set of flint arrowheads and a ring of red deer antlers from the largest bowl barrow, known as 'The Hunter's Barrow', and a cup, dagger, and the extraordinary bronze pin with a double-ring head which can be viewed in Devizes Museum, found in the largest bell barrow. During the 1950s many of the barrows were more extensively excavated by Nicholas Thomas and Charles Thomas. The final report is not yet available but will describe many extra burials and grave goods, as well as details of barrow structure and environmental information that could not be recovered by Hoare's nineteenth-century techniques. For instance, total excavation of the disc barrow which lies within the apex of the triangular layout revealed the central cremation pit that had been found by Colt Hoare, plus a second cremation and bronze awl within the central mound, two further cremations in a second mound, and a third cremation deposit to the west of the centre. The full results will form a classic example of how modern excavation can amplify the finds and interpretation made by the antiquarian excavators.

Until the full results are published, no clear sequence of cemetery development can be offered. However, some interesting observations on the spatial layout of the barrows may be put forward. The earliest barrows may have been the two almost parallel and adjacent rows of very small barrows which can be seen to the north-west side of the cemetery (**39**). These overlay the centre of an extensive area of earlier, probably domestic, activity. Following this the main groups of large Early Bronze Age barrows, incorporating many of special type, appear to have been laid out, or developed over time, in specific short rows. This phenomenon is similar to that deduced for the Poor Lot cemetery, but in the case of Snail Down the rows are much shorter. However, as at Poor Lot, the rows all seem to have a large bell barrow at one end. The sequences of the four main rows, working from west to east across the cemetery are bell, bowl, bowl, saucer; bell, disc, bowl, bowl; bell, bowl, bowl; and, finally, bell, double bell, bowl. Within the apex of the triangle lies the other disc barrow and one bowl, whilst further south lie two isolated barrows, one a bell barrow and the other a pond barrow, which is now destroyed. This last monument lay in the floor of the head of the dry valley (*see* **39**), and, as at Poor Lot, may have been the visual and ceremonial focus for the barrow cemetery as a whole. Many other large barrow cemeteries which have generally been described as 'linear' in nature in fact can be broken down into smaller components, each of which may have a separate linear or nucleated character. This is even true for some of the most famous of the linear cemeteries such as that on Normanton Down, just south of Stonehenge, which will be analysed in the next chapter, and for some of the major clusters of barrows and ring ditches that lie in the vicinity of major ceremonial monuments of Late Neolithic and Early Bronze Age date.

Sacred barrowscapes

The most famous example of barrows and barrow cemeteries clustering around a ceremonial monument is the area around Stonehenge, where both barrows and the focal henge survive as upstanding architectural features within the landscape. Aspects of this landscape will be discussed in the final chapter. Around other major henge sites the barrows are less concentrated, and many of them are ploughed flat, as around Avebury. But even here there are some impressive runs of surviving mounds associated with elements of the complex such as the Sanctuary (**47**). The contents of a Beaker barrow just

47 *Overton Hill, Wiltshire: barrows, The Sanctuary (located in the pale field), and the former Ridgeway Café.* (© Crown copyright. NMR)

to the north of this Overton Hill group was described in chapter 2 (page 38). Alternatively, as at Dorchester in Dorset, the major focus of ceremonial monuments and inner zones of barrows have been obliterated by agriculture and urban development while only the outer sets of barrow cemeteries, mainly ranged along the South Dorset Ridgeway, survive in part. However, in most cases, the monuments and the barrows have now all been ploughed flat and patterns of spatial relationships can be inferred mainly from air photographic evidence only. We shall be looking briefly at two examples of such ploughed chalkland barrowscapes — one in Dorset and one in Yorkshire — but first a site which has benefited from major excavation will be considered. This is the cemetery known as Barrow Hills, located on the second terrace of the Thames river gravels on the northern outskirts of Abingdon in Oxfordshire. The name is recorded in medieval times, but the mounds were probably levelled at a fairly early date: certainly none appear to have been dug into by antiquarian excavators.

The complex of ring ditches comprises two major alignments which run almost parallel to each other (**48**). The more continuous line of crop circles starts on the eastern (right hand) side of the air photograph. It is not visible in the two central fields but ends within the large circle just west of the tree-lined road. The second row includes the pair of ring ditches at the south-west margin of the photograph, the double ring in the centre and part of a ditch just visible south of the eastern end of the north alignment. Just west of the area covered in this photo lies the site of the Abingdon causewayed enclosure, excavated in the 1920s, '50s and '60s in advance of quarrying and housing developments. It was always thought that the remarkable Barrow Hills cemetery may have been sited in relation to this Neolithic monument, and the results of many decades of excavation have served to illuminate the spatial relationships in a very clear and stimulating manner.

Eleven of the ring ditches in the eastern sectors of the cemetery were excavated in the 1930s and 1940s, mainly by the Oxford University Archaeological Society, in advance of gravel quarrying. Then in the early 1980s, the whole of the western field, including the three ring ditches visible in figure **48**, an oval barrow of Neolithic date and all the areas in between were fully excavated by the Oxford Archaeological Unit. The remarkable results of all these excavations have been described, assessed and fully interpreted in a magnificent monograph that includes coloured plans and diagrams of excellent clarity. The recovery of a wide-ranging spread of dateable grave goods and other finds, and the extensive programme of radiocarbon dating has meant that it has been feasible to analyse the probable sequence of cemetery development in a way that has seldom been possible. Following careful assessment of the radiocarbon dates and diagnostic finds, Paul Garwood was able to devise a detailed system of site phasing. This starts in the Early Neolithic with the construction of the causewayed enclosure, itself of two phases, just west of a small stream, and a small rectangular enclosure which develops into an oval barrow covering a rich Neolithic double burial across the stream to the east. Further east again there was another deposit of various human bones arranged in a probable timber setting. In the later Neolithic, groups of pits were dug close to the oval barrow and a little to the south; these were filled with special deposits of pottery, and similar pottery also entered the tops of the partly filled ditches at the causewayed enclosure. In the next phase, four widely spaced graves containing male Beaker burials were arranged in a line running south-west to north-east from the more southerly group of Neolithic pits. Two were located in small ring ditches and all were probably originally covered with small mounds. However, the two major rows of barrows which developed next during the Early Bronze Age period were on a slightly different alignment. These major rows may have developed sequentially but it is possible that widely spaced monuments, as in the south row, were constructed first, followed by gradual but controlled infilling. Garwood was able to show that the more continuous northerly run of ring ditches was actually made up of three separate segments, each of four adjacent barrows, lying on slightly different alignments. Such a layout is reminiscent of the row patterns that have been described for the Lambourn, Poor Lot and Snail Down cemeteries above. But in the case of Barrow Hills, we also know the contents of many of the barrows, and it seems that rich

48 *Barrow Hills, Radley, Oxfordshire, viewed from the south.* (© Crown copyright. NMR)

graves were concentrated particularly in the westernmost segment of the north alignment, but towards the eastern end of the south alignment.

The two major alignments diverge slightly towards their eastern ends, such that the rows of former barrows would have defined a funnel-shaped avenue which, if entered from the north-east, would have led to two small central ring ditches, and thence to a large open space in front of the Neolithic oval barrow. Thus the lines of round barrows seem to have marked out a processional pathway, leading to a small circular mound from which the first clear view of the open arena, and of the archaic and ancestral Neolithic monuments could be experienced. No evidence for a late Neolithic henge monument has been forthcoming, but the circular empty space may have formed an arena within which ceremonies such as those acted out at henge monuments elsewhere might have been held. Certainly it is around such large circular earthwork structures that groups of round barrows tend to cluster, both in lowland situations such as Dorchester on Thames, just a little downstream from Barrow Hills in the Thames valley, or on the chalklands of Wessex or the Yorkshire Wolds.

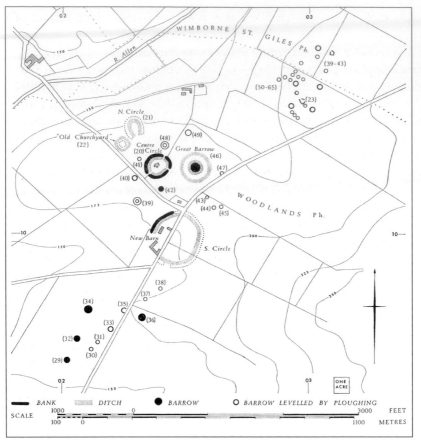

49 *Henge monuments and barrows at Knowlton, Dorset. (© Crown copyright. NMR)*

At Knowlton in Dorset a group of four henge monuments of varying size lie on a low spur overlooking the River Allen which runs a little north of the sites (**49** and **colour plate 17**). Only one of the enclosures, within which the ruined remains of the medieval church lie, survives fully as an earthwork; the others appear as cropmarks and are accompanied by further ring ditches of varying size and form. None of the barrows have been the subject of recorded antiquarian or modern excavation. Next to Church Henge lies a very large barrow, the mound of which is still extant, known as Great Barrow. This is equivalent in size to the giant barrows that occur in association with henge enclosures at Mount Pleasant (Conquer Barrow) or Marden in Wiltshire (the Hatfield Barrow, which is now ploughed flat), or to the massive Lanceborough King Barrow, near Maiden Castle, which will be discussed in the final chapter. The henges are not placed on a very prominent spur and the significance of the location is not appreciated until one visits the site and looks outward. From Church Henge it is clear that this position was chosen to give a full wide view down the main broad valley of the River Allen as it flows down towards its junction with the Stour at Wimborne, whilst also providing glimpses of a very important location up-river and on Cranborne Chase. For, looking north-east one sees clearly the high back profile of Penbury Knoll, a hill which Chris Tilley noted as of crucial visual importance in relation to the laying out of the Dorset Cursus, a Neolithic monument which runs across the ridged terrain of Cranborne Chase.

Amongst the henges at Knowlton there are further ring ditches, many of them visible on the air photograph (**colour plate 17**). These are well spaced out and do not form rows or clusters, but they do include several large monuments with double ditches which may be the remains of complex multi-phased or fancy styles of barrow. And several more examples of double and single ring ditches were recorded here during the dry summer of 1976. In the area to the south of the South Circle a second group of barrows appears to form a set of two alignments, one of which is completely ploughed out. These may have defined a processional way leading towards the henges, similar in function to that described above at Barrow Hills. North-east of the henges lies a third set of barrows. These are mainly smaller in size and cluster on the edge of the next spur. They also include a small rectilinear enclosure (23) and from here a very good view of the henge monuments can be experienced across the re-entrant side valley.

Returning to the Thames valley we shall next consider another complex of ceremonial and funerary monuments, that which lies around the site of the Devil's Quoits henge monument at Stanton Harcourt in Oxfordshire. This was largely contemporary with the barrow cemetery at Barrow Hills, but is completely different in terms of the major monuments represented and the layouts of round barrows around them. The two outstanding differences are that at the Devil's Quoits there was no Neolithic causewayed enclosure and no long barrows, whilst at Barrow Hills there was no major henge in the late Neolithic to Early Bronze Age period, only a roughly circular space. The complex south of Stanton Harcourt lies on a large expanse of gravel terrace bounded by the River Windrush and the Thames. The henge was excavated by Grimes in 1940, in advance of the construction of a wartime airfield, and subsequently by Margaret Gray and the Oxford Unit in the early 1970s and 1988. Some of the barrows and ring ditches which lie in the fields around, as at Barrow Hills, were excavated to varying extents, but mainly by the Oxford University Archaeological Society, in advance of gravel extraction. However, many others could not be excavated, so the resulting picture is patchy and incomplete (**50**).

The henge itself is of particular importance in that it is the only example with standing stones that is known from the Thames valley. The Big Rings henge at Dorchester on Thames was slightly larger, but the ring of stones at the Devil's Quoits marked it out as something very special, in a very special place. The stones were of a conglomerate that derives from the upper levels of the sands and gravels on and adjacent to the site. The recovery of one flint tool of Mesolithic date from the excavations, and a more substantial group from the area of Gravelly Guy nearby, indicates that this place was already frequented before Neolithic times. It may be that some of the conglomerate blocks were visible on the ground surface and that these strange pitted boulders had imbued the locality with a special significance for the hunting bands. Certainly by the Neolithic some monuments had been constructed — at least one Middle Neolithic barrow containing a burial with a jet belt slider and a row of two rectangular mortuary enclosures and a possible mini henge just east of the site of the Quoits. There is also widespread evidence of other later Neolithic activity in the form of pits containing varying styles of pottery scattered across the area west and north of the henge site (**50**). In other areas of the

Thames valley, such as Dorchester-on-Thames, alignments of mortuary enclosures and other small monuments became the precursors of the major linear earthwork phenomena of the Middle Neolithic, the cursus monuments. However, at Stanton Harcourt this did not happen.

Partly contemporary with these Neolithic activities came the intensive use of the area for ceremonial purposes. The henge was constructed, and around it a dense array of Beaker graves developed. These included some graves in existing or newly constructed barrows or ring ditch monuments, one of them within the ring ditch containing the Middle Neolithic burial, and a series of flat graves. Other Beaker material was recovered, as in the late Neolithic period, from pits without burials (**50**). There were also a small henge-like enclosure and a timber post ring located in the Gravelly Guy zone. A high proportion of the Beaker graves were quite rich, with daggers and stone wristguards as well as finely decorated Beaker vessels, and many of the burials were of adult men. These Beaker deposits and monuments seem to have then formed focal points for the establishment of small groups of ring ditches which then developed throughout the Early and Middle Bronze Age. Thus a wide range of Early Bronze Age burials and grave goods were recovered by excavation, and also several examples of the ring ditches were subsequently used for the interment of cremations in Middle Bronze Age urns (**50**). In comparison with the Beaker burials, the Early Bronze Age graves curiously contain few objects of note and the only rich grave group came from the sole major fancy barrow within the complex, a bell barrow known as the Stanton Harcourt Barrow. This contained a dagger, a miniature incense cup, a whetstone, a ring-headed bone pin and beads made from amber, jet and small fossil sponges.

The whole group of barrows and ring ditches arranged around the large henge and other smaller earthwork and timber monuments survived throughout the Iron Age period. During this time the ancient ceremonial area seems to have been preserved as pasture with arable land and settlements laid out around its margins, as described in the previous chapter. It was only in the early Roman period that the bank and ditch of the Devil's Quoits became subject to ploughing, and it is apparent that the stones themselves were not removed until the medieval period. Meanwhile most of the burial monuments had been ploughed flat, but interestingly the largest mound, the Stanton Harcourt bell barrow, with its rich contents, was not levelled until the eighteenth century, and still survived to a height of over half a metre when it was excavated in 1940.

The spatial arrangement of the ring ditches in the area around the Quoits could not be more different than that of the barrow cemetery at Barrow Hills. Instead of the strong linear groupings found at Barrow Hills there is a series of small clusters of ring ditches scattered across the landscape. The general clustering of the sites in this area into a set of five major groupings was first noticed and discussed by Humphrey Case. A more detailed consideration of the spacing of the ring ditches, by the simple method of joining each site to its nearest neighbour by a straight line, shows that the sites can be seen to form a series of much smaller groups, each including between two and seven ring ditches (**50**). All the small groups that include excavated sites contain burials of definite or probably Early Bronze Age date, and most also show evidence of earlier Beaker graves and Neolithic activity. Following a general idea first put forward by Case, these clusters can perhaps be

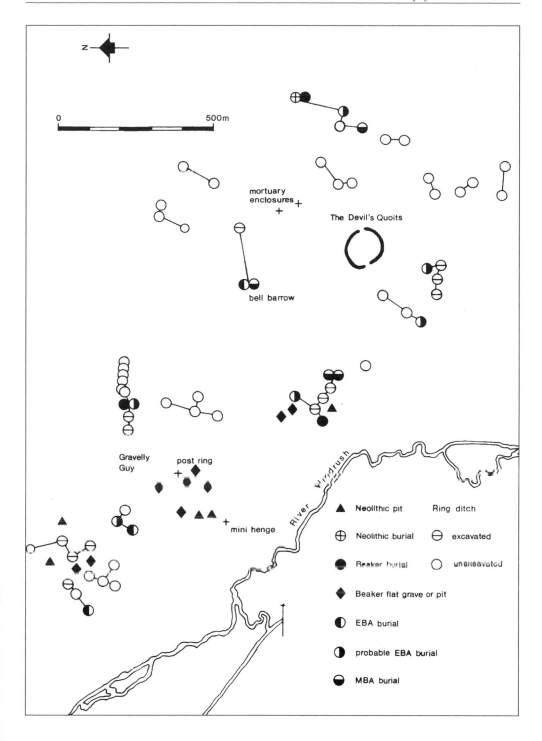

50 *Ring ditches around The Devil's Quoits, Stanton Harcourt, Oxfordshire.* (after Barclay, with additions)

interpreted as the burial grounds of different social groups who professed affiliation to the large henge monument. Some may have been the cattle farmers of the local gravel terraces, while others may have come from afar. Most of the mini groups show little evidence of strict internal structure, although there are two instances of short rows of contiguous rings. The large bell barrow, which may contain one of the latest Early Bronze Age graves lies in a relatively isolated position, north-west of the Quoits. Looking at the overall pattern it can be seen that the mini groups are arranged roughly in zones around two separate foci, firstly the Devil's Quoits itself, and secondly the smaller circular monuments and cluster of Beaker graves at Gravelly Guy. In both cases, the areas immediately around the ceremonial monuments are conspicuously clear of ring ditches. These zones seem to have been kept open, perhaps to function as arenas for specific enactments, similar in function to the circular space that was respected over so many centuries at Barrow Hills.

Finally we move north to Yorkshire to consider the relationships between barrows and monuments in the area around Rudston (**51**). The complex of Neolithic and Early Bronze Age monuments includes the henge monument known as Maidens Grave (**51**, G), sited on the floor of the Great Wold Valley, and the spectacular monolith which survives in the churchyard at Rudston (F). This standing stone, nearly 8m in height, stands on a significant bluff overlooking the point where the Gypsey Race river turns through a right angle to head east towards the sea at Bridlington. Most remarkable of all is the set of four Neolithic cursus monuments. The longest one (D) runs along the valley floor from high land to the north, while the other three (A, B and C) cross the valley from side to side in the vicinity of the river bend at Rudston. Barrows and ring ditches are not clustered around the henge, as we saw at Knowlton or the Devil's Quoits, but mainly at the upland terminals of the various cursus alignments (**51** and **52**). Some of these barrows may be of Neolithic date, and some may pre-date the construction of the cursus monuments, as is known in the case of the great Dorset Cursus. However, from those opened by Canon Greenwell in the nineteenth century, it was clear that most of the round barrows were erected over burials of Beaker and Early Bronze Age date. The date of the raising of the Rudston monolith is unknown, but it is likely to have been in place by the Bronze Age and to have been a key position for gatherings and ceremonies. It is sited on a bluff which provides a wonderful natural platform from which the cursus alignments and the groups of barrows could be viewed. Indeed, one could still view these monuments today if they had not been ploughed completely flat. However, the vistas can still be appreciated, and some impression may be gained from photographic images. **Colour plate 18** shows the line of view from the monolith to the west and up to the site of the terminal of cursus C and a major group of ring ditches located on the east-facing slope, and **colour plate 19** shows the author recording a similar vista to the south, this time encompassing the southern end of cursus A and the ridge-top siting of the barrows near Rudston Beacon. The views from the barrow zones towards the monolith were probably of at least equal significance in the past. Certainly, standing next to some of the barrows next to the south terminal of cursus A, a very fine view of the monolith can be obtained (**52** and **colour plate 20**). Although not clearly visible in the photograph, the stone stands next to the church tower which can be seen directly above the slight surviving mound of the barrow

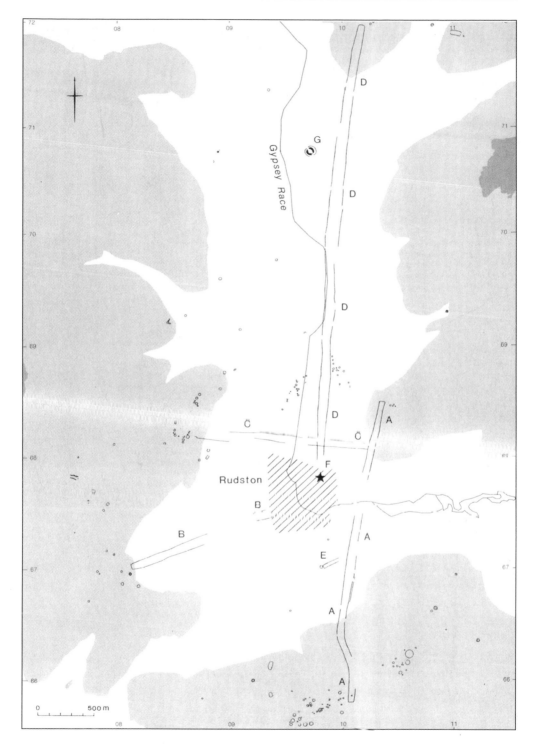

51 *Cursus monuments at Rudston, Yorkshire. Shading denotes land over 50m.*
(© Crown copyright. NMR)

52 *The south terminal of cursus A at Rudston, Yorkshire, viewed from the south, with ring ditches of ploughed barrows in the same field.* (© Crown copyright. NMR)

in the foreground. This area seems to have been a primary focus for pit deposition and barrow construction throughout the Late Neolithic and Early Bronze Age periods, and the reason for this may have been connected to the topography and to visibility. We have seen that this spot commands a fine view into the Great Wold Valley and towards the monolith; if one turns the other way then a stunning contrasting view of the North Sea is revealed. Furthermore, both of these striking vistas would have been apparent even if the land was still heavily forested. On returning from Yorkshire, I was checking through the accounts of nineteenth-century barrow excavations near Rudston and was excited to discover that Canon Greenwell, writing in 1877, had perceived a similar interpretation for the siting of the barrows that lie near to the end of cursus A:

> The position which the barrows occupy is a very striking one, and must always
> have been so. The men who raised these funeral mounds looked on the one
> side over the swelling upland of the wold, bleak, grey, and treeless, their eye

taking in on many a distant ridge the burial-places of chiefs of other, though perhaps kindred, tribes: whilst upon an outcrop of rock, lifting itself out of the valley just beneath them, rose the lofty monolith which now stands in Rudstone churchyard . . . There it stood, telling them perchance that at its base was laid to rest a mightier warrior than him they were entombing on the height above; or it may have spoken to them as the symbol of a belief, according to which their lives were regulated, and marked the place it stood upon as holy ground. If they looked to the south there was nothing but a dreary tract of marsh-land, which seemed almost interminable, wherein however, amidst the coarse vegetation and brushwood, the deer and wild swine had their haunt, and where the beaver made a habitation almost equal in point of construction to those they had themselves the skill to form. Beyond was the sea, as yet enlivened by no sail.

While the contemporary reader might baulk at the Victorian attitudes to politics and gender, and the presumed primitive nature of prehistoric people, enshrined in this passage, the impression of view and landscape that was experienced by Greenwell is remarkably similar to that which can be perceived at the present day. The general theme of barrows in a visual landscape will be taken up again in the final chapter, but before that we shall take a closer look at some of the groups of grave goods that were placed in the Early Bronze Age round barrows of Britain.

Notes

Andrew Fleming's definitions of cemetery types are in Fleming 1971, using the data from Grinsell 1957 (Wiltshire) and 1959 (Dorset). For the studies of barrow locations in Wales and south-east England see Roese 1981 and Field 1998, also Tomalin 1993 and 1996.

Small nucleated cemeteries. West Heath: Drewett *et al* 1988, 75 and 80-84 for a summary and full references, Roxton: Taylor and Woodward 1985.

Linear cemeteries. The Five Marys: Grinsell 1959, 98; Ashen Hill: Grinsell 1971, 98, Chewton Mendip barrows 5 to 12.

Dispersed cemeteries. Stanton Moor: Barnatt and Smith 1997, figure 16 for summary plan; Brenig: Lynch 1993, figure **44** is based on her figure 1.1; Lambourn Seven Barrows: Case 1957 and Wymer 1964, figure **45** is based on Case 1957, figure 1, plus additions.

Row cemeteries. Poor Lot: RCHM 1970, 460; Winterbourne Steepleton pond barrow: Atkinson et al 1951; Snail Down: Thomas and Thomas 1959.

Sacred barrowscapes. Barrows around Avebury: Malone 1989, figure 5, around Stonehenge: Woodward and Woodward 1996; Barrow Hills: Barclay and Halpin 1999; Knowlton: RCHM 1975, 113-116; Devil's Quoits: Barclay et al 1995, figure **50** is based on their figure 39, with additions, Case 1982. Rudston: Stoertz 1997, Greenwell and Rolleston 1877.

5   Barrows and exotic substances

The occurrence of exotic substances with burials in barrows dates back to the time of the earliest individual interments during the late Neolithic period. In chapter 2 we saw that curious items such as sea shells, the polished teeth from wild animals, and pieces of shining white quartz were being placed with human bones inside stone chambered long barrows in the west, and in earthen round mounds such as that at Duggleby Howe in Yorkshire. A little later, this inventory of exotic materials was suddenly and dramatically enhanced by the first appearance in Beaker graves of specially designed items crafted in gold, coloured polished stones, jet and amber. The earliest objects of jet may be the sliders found in certain graves of later Neolithic date, but the main expansion of the use of jet, amber, and highly polished bone and coloured stone items occurs around the turn of the Late Neolithic and Early Bronze Age periods. At this time various forms of belt rings, buttons, earrings, polished stone battle-axes and archers' wristguards begin to be found, alongside the continuing deposition of special items made from antlers and boars' tusks, and the results of the newest technological developments: the first copper daggers.

Most of these categories of finds have been studied separately by different archaeologists. The main aim of this chapter is to consider their important role and possible interpretations that can be put upon the use of all these exotic raw materials. This will partly be achieved by some unusual but very straightforward methods of study. Such methods will include consideration of how the objects might have been perceived by the people who were wearing or using them, through detailed studies of colour and texture. They also encompass assessments of the state of condition and 'completeness' of objects in grave groups in order to provide clues to the possible function of the items in everyday and ceremonial life during the Early Bronze Age.

Stone wristguards

As an introductory sample, we shall briefly consider the archers' wristguards found with certain Beaker burials. Very few wristguards are actually known from barrows, all the others being stray finds. Only 14 were listed in Clarke's Beaker catalogue of 1970, and only a few have been excavated since, but they occur widely from north Scotland to southern Britain. In terms of sensual perception, the main characteristics of the wristguards are that they are very thin, highly polished and often made from brightly coloured stone. Thus there are three that are blue, four in shades of green, and two of shiny black. Furthermore, three of them are embellished with gold-capped rivets covering the attachment holes. It has been noted in general that wristguards in Britain and Europe were made from a wide range of special and rare stones including jasper, porcellanite, steatite and porphyrite. Interestingly, in comparison with the examples noted above, the preferred colours in continental Europe and in Ireland were red and grey. The main problem arising from attempts to study colour and texture is that these aspects are seldom recorded in archaeological descriptions. Therefore to gather the information on the specific items discussed above it was necessary to view afresh the actual pieces in the museum collections within which they are housed. A similar problem relates to any study of wear patterns and fragmentation. Again the relevant data has rarely been published and recourse to the actual objects is necessary. Stone wristguards show little signs of wear, and it is generally felt that they were special items worn for display only. However, several of them were deposited in the grave in a broken state. At Barnack, the corner of the wristguard had been deliberately detached, but then replaced in position. But in three other cases, corners were completely missing, and many of the stray finds are broken pieces. Here we may be seeing evidence of a rite which involved both the defusing of the power of these highly charged symbolic items prior to burial, as well as for the interesting possibility that small fragments from them may have been kept as heirlooms or tokens by descendants or other associates of the deceased.

The Wessex Culture

Having introduced some aspects of a new and exciting method of looking at grave goods made from special substances, we shall now turn to a detailed reconsideration of some of the most famous items from Bronze Age graves in Britain. Most of them derive from the groups of well preserved and often visited round barrows which cluster around Stonehenge and which belong to the so-called Wessex Culture (**53**). The idea of a Wessex Culture was first expounded by Stuart Piggott in a brilliant paper which was printed in 1938. He was able to pinpoint a fairly confined group of barrow graves, many of which had been excavated by Colt Hoare and Cunnington in the nineteenth century and contained objects of great rarity and richness. Through detailed study of various different categories of object: bronze axes and daggers, dagger hafts ornamented with gold, special types of miniature pot, gold objects, faience beads, amber, exotic pendants, bronze pins and 'sceptres', and by comparing these with similar material in Brittany and beyond, Piggott was able to suggest the existence of a Wessex Culture which he interpreted in the following terms:

> The nature of the evidence — finds from the richly-furnished graves of chieftains — presents us with a view of the material equipment of an aristocratic minority. The basic folk culture appears . . . to have been similar to the food-vessel culture of the greater part of Britain . . . but in Wessex there was, superimposed on this somewhat uninteresting and unenterprising substratum, an intrusive ruling class whose delight in barbaric finery led them to open trade connections not only with their Breton homeland, but with central Europe and Scandinavia . . .

This idea of a wealthy chieftain-led society based on long-distance trade links has prevailed for over sixty years. Most scholarly studies of the material have been undertaken by researchers who specialise in a particular category of material: the bronze daggers,

53 *Hoare's bird's eye view of the barrow group at Lake, near Stonehenge. (© Crown copyright. NMR)*

goldwork, faience beads or amber (*see* **54**, also **58**, **59** and **60**). Some of this research has centred on technological matters, how the objects were made and where the raw materials came from, but most effort has been concentrated on elucidation of a relative chronology for the various types of grave good and for the grave groups. A general division into two successive groups of grave: Wessex I and Wessex II is still current, although some problems remain. And, when the possibility of some graves containing heirloom items, which may have been in circulation for centuries, is taken into account, the feasibility of constructing any detailed time sequence for the graves must be doubted. However, with the general chronological pattern in place, it is possible to proceed to a consideration of some other far reaching questions. How long had the items in any one grave been in circulation, what were they used for, what is the meaning of the recurring combinations of different objects, and who used them? Recently Mike Parker Pearson has pointed out that the Wessex chieftain theory may be incorrect. The burial of rich objects within barrows could well

54 *Gold pommel from a dagger hilt. Found in Edward Cunnington's Ridgeway barrow 7: Weymouth G8, Dorset.* (©: Dorset Natural History and Archaeological Society)

have *prevented* the accumulation of wealth and power through inheritance in aristocratic families, and the deposition of so much richness in the graves may have been designed specifically as a striking display of social standing within the community. Society may have been an amalgam of family-based groups roughly equal in status but where differences in individual social standing were played out through the wearing of visible emblems or exotic equipment and the conspicuous disposal of valuable goods. It can now be understood that Piggott's original exclusively hierarchical and militaristic model of Early Bronze Age society in Wessex may have been influenced by the political and militaristic ambience current in this country between the World Wars. In this same twentieth-century context, Sir Mortimer Wheeler was writing his intensely evocative narrative reconstruction of Vespasian's attack on the Iron Age hillfort at Maiden Castle. However more recent research and excavation has shown that this simple militaristic interpretation was only one extreme reading of the complex and sometimes ambiguous archaeological evidence.

Wessex barrows

As far as the barrows are concerned, it is generally held that Wessex graves are closely associated with fancy barrows, that the richest grave groups cluster around Stonehenge and that there was a clear gender distinction. Thus in Wessex I a group of rich male burials with daggers, goldwork and other regalia are contrasted with a few rich female graves associated with pendants of gold, bronze and amber. In the Wessex II stage cremation became the preferred rite, no more goldwork was deposited but there was a similar division between male warrior graves with daggers, bronze pins and whetstones, and female burials

55 The Normanton Down barrow group, Wiltshire, viewed from the south-east in 1980.
(© Crown copyright. NMR)

containing mixtures of beads which now included items made from faience. Bell barrows are seen as having been constructed primarily for male burials, while women were interred in disc barrows. Unfortunately, almost all of these statements can be questioned. Firstly, there is no very close correlation between the richness of grave groups and barrow type. A study of the burials in the main barrow cemeteries around Stonehenge has shown that well over half of the graves with Wessex grave goods (62%) were placed under simple bowl barrows, although 52% of the very rich and wealthy groups come from bell or disc barrows. The general pattern can be illustrated by considering the layout of one such cemetery — the extended linear group on Normanton Down (**55** and **56**). Amongst the barrows where records of the excavated contents have survived, several of the fancy barrows contained cremations alone, while seven out of the twelve Wessex grave groups, including the very wealthy finds from Bush Barrow, derive from bowl barrows, some of which are relatively small in size.

56 *The Normanton Down barrow group: barrow types and burial contents.* (©: Exon, Gaffney, Woodward and Yorston)

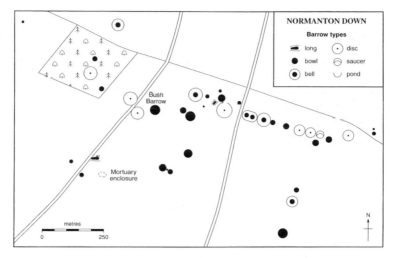

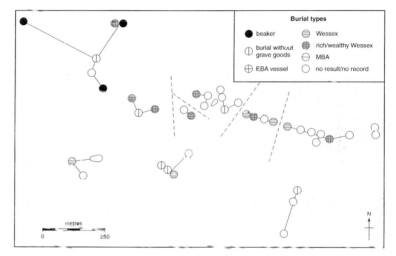

The second point is that very few of the exceptionally rich graves occur near to Stonehenge (**colour plate 21**). Two of them do, but the other candidates are widely spread across the country and occur as single barrows, usually simple bowls, rather than in cemeteries. Examples include Rillaton on Bodmin Moor (*see* **31**), Hameldon on Dartmoor, Hove on the Sussex coastal plain, Radwell in Bedfordshire and Little Cressingham in Norfolk. At Clandon in Dorset, the large bowl barrow covered a deposit of rich and exotic items (**58-60** and **62**; **colour plate 5**), but they were not associated with a grave, and any primary burial or burials were not reached by the excavator (*see* **21**). The barrow occurs alone, sitting in an isolated position on the end of a whale-backed hill, the other end of which is occupied by the causewayed enclosure and bank barrow which predate the Iron Age hillfort of Maiden Castle (**colour plate 22**).

Thirdly, the matter of sex and gender must be reviewed. As most of the burials were excavated by Colt Hoare and other antiquarians, who did not retrieve the human remains, there is no chance of deducing the age and sex of any of the cremations recovered. In

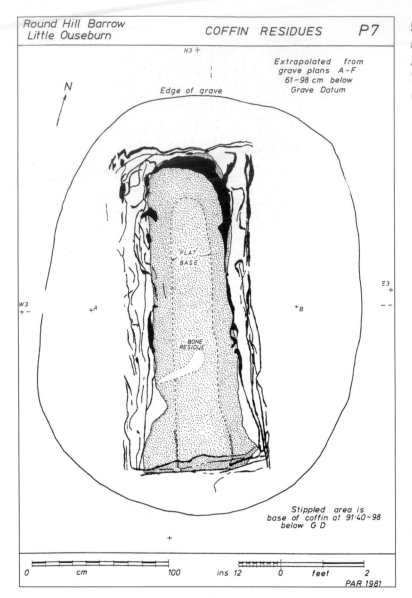

Round Hill Barrow
Little Ouseburn

COFFIN RESIDUES   P7

N3 +

N

Edge of grave

Extrapolated from
grave plans A~F
61~98 cm below
Grave Datum

FLAT
BASE

W3
+ –

+A

+B

53
+

– –

BONE
RESIDUE

Stippled area is
base of coffin at 91·40~98
below G D

+

0   cm   100   ins 12   0   feet   2

PAR 1981

57 *Traces of a wooden coffin at Little Ouseburn, Yorkshire.* (©: Philip Rahtz)

several cases of twentieth-century excavation, it has been found that soil conditions have caused the bones to have decayed completely. In such circumstances, other detail such as the outlines of a wooden coffin may be retrievable (**57**), but again the age and sex of the person interred must remain elusive. Where actual skeletal remains are concerned there is a major problem. The bones were not kept by Colt Hoare, nor were they described and analysed in the detailed way that was achieved by the antiquarians investigating barrows on the Yorkshire Wolds. And where identifications of the age and sex of a few cremations from recently excavated disc barrows have been made it has been shown that several of them were not women, but men. The generalised male/female identifications attributed to the various Wessex grave groups have in fact been deduced

58 *Fragmentary amber cup from the Clandon Barrow.* (©: Dorset Natural History and Archaeological Society)

from the grave goods. The simple assertions that daggers denote men and jewellery denotes women are not acceptable within modern research. They are negated by much anthropological evidence and form yet another legacy from workers practising in the inter-war and immediate post-war years — a time when gender roles in Great Britain were very heavily defined. Obviously, the time has come for the whole body of material to be studied afresh, casting away the existing premises and looking at the primary evidence in some different ways.

The tentative beginnings of such a new study will be attempted by considering the two aspects that were investigated in relation to Beaker wristguards — the assessment of sensual perception and the question of use-wear and fragmentation. As well as the visual perception of colour and tactile experience of texture we shall also refer to sound, taste and smell. In the sphere of fragmentation we shall be looking at objects which were deliberately broken and items which are merely parts of larger things or composite entities. We shall also be defining particular sets of material equipment. At Clandon, where the description by Edward Cunnington is rather more detailed than those made by Colt Hoare in relation to the diggings of his great uncle William Cunnington on Salisbury Plain, we know that the dagger, the amber cup (**58**) and the small accessory cup (**62**) were all broken into pieces before they were deposited. Most of the bits seem to have been present, except for part of the bronze dagger blade, which may have been deliberately removed. The gold lozenge (**59**) and the jet macehead with gold bosses (**60**) on the other hand were buried intact, although no human bones were present. Microscopic study of the gold lozenge, and of related items from Wessex graves elsewhere, has shown two things. Firstly, many of the gold items appear to have been

59 *Gold lozenge from the Clandon Barrow.*
(©: Dorset Natural History and Archaeological Society)

60 *Jet mace-head with gold inserts from the Clandon Barrow.*
(©: Dorset Natural History and Archaeological Society)

made by a single hand, or by a very closely knit school of craftsmen, and, secondly, the pieces are not at all worn. This suggested to the analysts that all these gold objects may have been made and deposited in a very short period of time. However, there are other possible explanations: the objects were very carefully stored in soft coverings, they were displayed only briefly at special ceremonies and festivals, and, finally, that they may have been handed down as heirlooms or powerful pieces of ritual equipment within family or other social groups. If such a theory of ritual dependence on heirloom items is accepted, then the detailed dating of grave groups in terms of the inferred date of manufacture of the constituent elements can no longer be accepted. Until a detailed study of the wear patterns and potential function of all the categories of items in a large number of graves has been undertaken, it seems wiser to treat all the graves together as a single entity for analysis, and it is on this basis that the following studies have been attempted.

Exotic substances

Certain raw materials have been regarded as special and precious by human populations over many millennia and in many different parts of the world. The nature of such substances was reviewed by Grahame Clark in his book *Symbols of Excellence*. This book has the interesting subtitle *Precious materials as expressions of status* and defines the materials as those which display a particularly attractive colour and surface appearance. They may also possess unusual physical properties, are generally rare, obtainable only from a few distant sources, and usually have no everyday useful function. Up to the end of the Bronze Age in Europe, the main precious substances that were in use were ivory and shell, amber, jadeite and gold. Ivory, from the tusks of elephant, mammoth, walrus or sperm whale has been in use for charms, ornaments and figurines since Palaeolithic times. Its pleasing creamy white colour and smooth, fine-grained texture, together with its durability, are its main properties. These properties could be achieved to some extent by the use of bone and antler or could be copied by the use of certain marine shells, such as *Spondylus gaederopus*, which became popular for the manufacture of ornaments in Neolithic Europe. Also very important were cowrie shells, the shape of which can be seen to resemble on the one hand, a vulva, or on the other, the human eye. This species was much prized and cowrie shells from the Indian Ocean are known from Upper Palaeolithic graves in the south of France. Jade was most commonly revered in areas where good sources were reasonably accessible, especially in China and in Aztec Mexico. As well as possessing a fine appearance, jade also has medical and even musical properties. Polished jadeite axes, probably using raw material from Switzerland or north Italy, were valued in Neolithic Britain and Europe, but this material had gone out of use by the Bronze Age. It may have been supplanted by objects made from amber and gold.

Amber is renowned for its smoothness, colour range and warmth of touch. In historic times its therapeutic properties have also often received mention. Hippocrates recommended amber oil as a stimulant, for the relief of asthma, or as a liniment for chest complaints, and Dr Joan Evans recorded that, in 1922 Mayfair, amber necklaces were still being sold as curatives for croup, whooping cough and asthma. It can also be used as incense, but its one outstanding proven physical property is its electrical qualities. When rubbed with certain materials such as textiles or fur, significant electrostatic energy is released. Amber, obtained mainly from marine locations in the Baltic, but also from the eastern shores of Britain, was used to make figurines, beads and amulets in the Mesolithic, and by the later Neolithic and Early Bronze Age was widely in use, mainly for the production of composite crescent-shaped necklaces incorporating spacer beads with complex ornamental borings. Jet possesses a dense, velvety black colour and a resinous lustre which can be enhanced by polishing. Like amber, it can be electrified by rubbing and is sometimes known as 'black amber'. The best British source of jet is at Whitby in Yorkshire — material from this location was used for ornaments and accessories from the late Neolithic, and throughout the Bronze Age and Early Iron Age in the north. Recent analyses have shown that many of the black items from the Wessex graves of Wiltshire are also made from Yorkshire jet, although the slightly less dense black shale from Purbeck in Dorset was also employed in the manufacture of ornaments.

Gold always seems to have been revered above all other precious substances. The main appeal is its unique colour and lustre, the fact that it never tarnishes and that it possesses some useful physical properties: its extreme malleability means that it can be formed into very thin sheets and pulled to form fine wire. Also, of all the exotic substances available in prehistory, gold was the most rare. Mention must also be made here of faience, although of course this is not a naturally occurring substance. Faience is a glass-like material with a separate glazed surface coloured by traces of copper compounds to provide a bright turquoise blue coloration. Interestingly, some of the earliest precious stones to have been used in the world were those displaying similarly striking shades of blue. These are lapis lazuli and turquoise, both of which were being used in the Near East by about 3000 BC, and in ancient Egypt faience was often used in association with these blue stones, or to replace them. Only about 250 faience beads are known from Britain. It used to be thought that some of them, especially the segmented variety, were imports from the Mediterranean world, but recent interpretations of the scientific analyses carried out suggest that most probably all were made locally. Some of the types, such as the star- and quoit-shaped beads, are mainly found in Scotland and it is likely that this is where those types at least were manufactured.

Finally, the question of perishable exotic substances must be considered. Throughout the world, some of the organic items which are recurrently collected and revered as emblems of status are highly coloured furs and feathers. The remains of such materials have seldom been recovered in archaeological deposits in Britain, but a hint that such things may have been highly significant is provided by the evidence of animal pelts used in the manufacture of composite sheaths or scabbards. Traces of skin and fur have been identified from scabbards found in Early Bronze Age graves in various parts of the country, but notably in Scotland. Other exotic materials incorporated in the sheaths and hilts of such daggers are special woods, animal horn and sperm whale ivory. It has seldom been possible to identify the skin or leather components to species, but where this has been achieved the fibres seem to have derived from oxen or the European bison (aurochs). No doubt the skins of wild animals which displayed particular coloration or tonal effects, such as those from fox, badger, beaver, wolf or wild pig, would also have been particularly prized.

Objects from rich Early Bronze Age graves which are made from gold, amber, jet and faience are generally well known. However, there are many other items within the grave groups that have never been studied in detail. These are the objects made from stone, bone and shell. Some of the pieces, such as the polished oval macehead from Bush Barrow, and a few shaft-hole axes, or the finely pressure-flaked arrowheads, have been discussed, but there are many more items that require scientific analysis. There are frequent occurrences of stone objects, often exotically coloured and polished, which have been described as whetstones or arrow straighteners. Some other possible functions for such items will be considered later; here we are most interested in their colours and textures which are highly specific and, it is suggested, deliberately selected. In addition to the stone items, there is a wide variety of objects — pins, pendants, tweezers, rings, beads and plaques, made from highly polished bone, animal teeth and tusks, which are often perforated, shells from riverine and marine sources, and small fossils with interesting shapes. There are also less frequent occurrences of highly exotic geological substances such as quartz crystals, 'marcasite', haematite, rock crystal and stalactite. Amongst this wealth of bright, smooth, shiny and eye-catching objects the most exotic of all are those pieces which combine the use of several different substances within their manufacture. These include the amber discs with gold bindings, complex pendants made from amber, gold and bronze, and the highly exotic macehead from the Clandon Barrow (**60**). This is a large polished block of black jet. Cut into it there are five circular sockets which originally contained removable plugs of shale with slightly conical caps, topped with thin covers of gold foil. Of these five sockets, only four retain their shale inserts, and only two of the gold covers and fragments of a third survive. Underneath is an irregular hole for the attachment of a shaft, which may have been made from wood.

The overriding features that seem to be characteristic of all the items selected for inclusion in the rich Wessex graves are those relating to colour and texture. The objects, when first buried, were all brightly coloured, shiny, lustrous, smooth, mainly cool to the touch, and neatly shaped. In order to assess these aspects, a record was made of the colour and texture of all the Wessex grave goods on display in Devizes Museum. The results of this study are presented in figure **61**. Obviously some of the pieces will have lost their original colours or surface effects due to natural decay in the soil. This particularly applies to pieces of bronzework. These now look brown or blue-green but of course would originally have presented highly polished red-gold or silvery surfaces. For the calculations summarised in figure **61**, all items were given a value of one, except for beads, where each group of beads of a single raw material was counted as one: for instance, six faience beads and nine amber beads gives values of one blue and one red. The most preferred colour by far is gold or silver. This mainly includes items of metalwork, gold and bronze, but a wide variety of objects are included ranging from weapons and tools through to beads, pendants, belt hooks and symbolic emblems. The preponderance of the colour red, mainly amongst items of amber but also including certain stone beads, a Breton handled pot, haematite nodules and some of the polishing stones, may also cause little surprise. What may be of more interest is that the next most commonly occurring colours are black and white. The black category mainly consists of items made from shale and jet or

barrow Grinsell numbers	gold silver	red orange	black dark grey	gold/ black; gold/ red	white cream	blue	brown	green	DMC Nos.
Wilsford									
G3		1	1			1			390-5
G5	6				3	2	1		168-78
G7	2	4	2				1		147-58
G8	3	7		3					179-92
G16		1	1						308-12
G23	3		1		1				163-7
G42	2	2			2				364
G46		1				1	1		337-9
G56	2				1		1		159-62
G58	2				3+		1	1	211-8
Ames-bury G48		1			1	1			399-405
Durring-ton G47			2			1			334-6
Winter-bourne Stoke									
G4	2				3				219-24
G5	3	1			1				263-6
G8	2	1			5	2			300-5
G14		1							291-8
G68			1			1			455-61
Milston G3 or 7	2		1						361-2
Preshute G1a	6	4	1	2	1		1		195-210
Upton Lovell									
G1		1	3			1			340-2
G2a	1	1	5		15		4	2	242-62
G2e	7	1							225-33
Totals	43	27	18	5	36	10	10	3	

61 *Finds from Wessex barrows housed in Devizes Museum, classified according to colour, (DMC denotes Devizes Museum Catalogue 1964)* polished other stones, whilst the creamy white objects are the myriad items made from bone and shell mentioned earlier, plus beads made from chalk and items of other white stones including some of the flint tools and 'whetstones'. The brown items, including various battle axes, polishing stones and fossils, may have been selected for their shapes and textures rather than basic colour, but the blue and green objects, mainly faience but also incorporating various polished stone pieces, would have stood out in strong contrast to the predominant red/gold and black/white schemes apparent amongst the individual assemblages. In many different human societies around the world, some basic colour contrasts are associated with similar symbolic meanings. The most common examples are the correlation of the colour red with blood and danger, flesh and fertility; black with darkness and death. White often denotes bones, hardness and light but can also be connected to human milk. Thus white may mean female against red which signifies male. Whether any such symbolism is reflected in the Wessex grave assemblages is not yet clear. Red and black or red and white items often occur together, although black and white combinations are rare.

Peculiar substances

The title of this section has deliberately been taken from the subtitle to Andrew Sherratt's introduction to a book which discusses aspects of psychoactive substances in history and anthropology. In that book, and in a series of earlier papers, Sherratt has argued not only that the use of psychoactive substances — alcohol, aromatics, drugs and hallucinogens — has been widespread since the very beginnings of human prehistory, but that also they have performed a crucial component of many everyday and more exclusive social activities. The dependence on alcohol within Europe dates only from the Early Bronze Age, when the spread of particular styles of handled drinking cups spread north and westwards from the wine drinking areas of the eastern Mediterranean. In north Europe however, the beverages more likely consisted of strange mixtures of mead and mixed fruit wines, laced with opiates and imbibed from the different styles of decorated Beaker vessels which occur from Czechoslovakia to Ireland. Prior to this, Sherratt has argued that the pattern of use of psychoactive substances in temperate Europe resembled more that of the native North American Indians, 'it being essentially a zone of smoking cultures rather than drinking cultures'. But the early inhabitants of north Europe were not smoking tobacco, of course. The opium poppy is native to the Mediterranean zone and was grown by the earliest Neolithic farmers of central Europe. Seed capsules are known from Neolithic deposits in Spain and Switzerland and it seems likely that it was an opiate that was burned in the special pottery braziers, otherwise called vase supports, that are found from Neolithic sites in western Europe. In addition to this group of substances, there is convincing evidence that the usage of hemp seed, cannabis, to produce vapours for inhalation was widespread around the Black Sea, and at points further east, probably since at least the beginning of the Neolithic. These practices also involved the use of footed pottery braziers and these have been found in graves along with the remains of pouches containing hemp seeds. The habit undoubtedly spread to Europe where cannabis may have been infused as well as smoked, and drunk in combination with the fruity alcoholic concoctions described above.

The miniature vessels found in many Early Bronze Age graves in Britain are commonly known as incense cups, and it is highly probable that they were used not only to burn aromatic materials but also in the releasing of psychoactive smoke from opium or cannabis. The cups occur in various styles, the most famous being the Grape Cups and Aldbourne Cups described in Piggott's original 1938 paper, but all are characterised by some key features. They tend to be vessels with incurving rims rather than open bowls or dishes, and some of them have lids; often the walls are perforated with rows of holes or cut-outs, or smaller numbers of circular holes, and they often display signs of burning. Recent observations in museum collections indicate that residues of burnt materials adhere to the insides of some of the vessels, but to my knowledge none of these have been scientifically analysed. Many of the vessels are decorated with complex schemes of geometric decoration similar to those which occurs on some of the bronze and gold items found in the graves (**62**). The cups seem to have been designed specifically for the controlled burning of substances. Some have suspension loops, and these as well as the sets of perforations would have allowed the cup to be strung up, perhaps within a confined space such as a tent. This also would have allowed the schemes of decoration, which often extend on to the bottom of the pot, to be fully appreciated. The pairs of perforated holes that occur on large numbers of the cups have usually been interpreted as symbolic eye motifs, but it seems likely that they had a practical function as well. It may be that they were intended to hold strings or fibres, primarily to allow suspension of the cup from a person's waist, or to facilitate the swinging of the cup. This action, as in the usage of censers in churches, increases the level of burning and smoke production, and can involve the spinning of a vessel in either a horizontal or vertical plane, the contents of the vessel being held safely in place by centrifugal force.

Although some of the most elaborate types of accessory cup come mainly from Early Bronze Age graves in Wessex, the type as a whole occurs commonly throughout Britain. No full catalogue of these fascinating vessels has ever been prepared, but the listing of those found with Collared Urns provides a good impression of their countrywide distribution and features. Of the 33 Wessex examples in Devizes Museum, most (82%) are decorated. Of these, 59% are also perforated. The plain cups are less often perforated and the same observation can be applied to the 60 cups found with Collared Urns, amongst which 45% are plain and mainly not perforated. Of the 33 cups with Collared Urns that do carry decoration, 45% are also perforated. The point of these simple statistics is to demonstrate that although the use of perforated and highly decorated miniature cups was concentrated in Wessex, their use was very widespread and occurred at a significant level right across Britain. If, as has been argued, their primary use was for the production of psychoactive fumes then this activity was taking place in Scotland, north Wales, Yorkshire and East Anglia as well as on Salisbury Plain.

Special substances, whether aromatic leaves and bark, resins or hemp seed, need special preparation prior to burning. Strike-a-lights of flint or iron pyrites are fairly common in the grave assemblages. One class of items which may have been used in the chopping and grinding of substances are the small bronze knives, the most elaborate of which is that with an amber hilt terminal from the Manton Barrow (Preshute G1a) on the Marlborough Downs. Some of the so-called whetstones, many of which are perforated for suspension,

62 *Pottery cup from the Clandon Barrow.*
(©: Dorset Natural History and Archaeological Society)

and made from special stone types, may have served as cutting blocks or palettes. Bone tweezers may also have been used in the cutting and handling of the substances, although a cosmetic function has generally been assumed. But the removal of body hair may have been undertaken for, or during, rituals. The stone palettes might have been used also for the mixing of ointments, body paint and cosmetics, and the finely pointed bronze awls, which are traditionally associated with leather working, may have been used for tattooing.

In sensory terms, most of the discussion so far has concentrated on the visual aspects of colour and texture and the possible assault on the senses of taste and smell caused by the burning of various substances. It remains to consider whether there is any evidence surviving from these graves which might relate to the production of special sounds or noises. It is likely that a main component of ceremonial activities would have been dancing and song, orchestrated by complex systems of drumming. There is no clear evidence for drums in the British Bronze Age — presumably such instruments were made from perishable materials such as wood and animal skins, sinews and bladders — although ceramic examples are known from eastern Europe. However, there are two items made from bronze which have sets of loose rings and may have functioned as 'jangles'. One is a pin from one of the barrows on Snail Down, Wiltshire, and the other is a curious two-pronged object from Wilsford barrow G58, in the Wilsford group near Stonehenge. This object is elaborately decorated and has a set of three interlocking loose rings attached to it. The only other type of possible musical equipment is the whistle. There is one probable example, made from the leg bone of a swan, from one of the rich grave groups on Normanton Down (Wilsford G23), and three bone whistles have been found with

Collared Urns, from Edinburgh, Snailwell in Cambridgeshire and Baildon, West Yorkshire. Such instruments probably form part of a very long-lived tradition of whistles, early examples of which, made from the foot bones of oxen, are known from Neolithic contexts at Skara Brae on Orkney, Lower Dounreay, Caithness and the West Kennet chambered long barrow near Avebury.

Beads

In terms of total numbers, the most common form of object found in rich Early Bronze Age graves are beads. As we have seen, these may be made from gold, amber, jet, shale, faience, bone, stone, clay, shells or fossils. They are brightly coloured and, although small, are distinctly eye-catching. These beads have traditionally been interpreted as the components of the necklaces of wealthy women who were buried under the mini mounds within disc barrows. However, very few complete or near-complete necklaces have ever been found. There are no significant groups of faience beads at all and, as stated above, there are only a total of about 250 such beads from the country as a whole. Of amber, there are substantial portions of necklaces from the Golden Barrow at Upton Lovell (G2e), from Little Cressingham in Norfolk and from a barrow in the Lake group near Stonehenge (Wilsford G47,49 or 50) — and that is all. Two of these are multi-strand necklaces, with the individual strings of beads kept apart by flat spacer plates; these have complex patterns of borings through which the strings passed. Otherwise there are just small numbers of amber beads, often associated with various other beads made from different materials, or deposits of single, or just a few, bored spacer plates. As David Tomalin has noted, some spacer plates may have been in circulation as individual heirlooms for a very long time. Such spacer plates are often broken and very worn. Much the same applies for the crescentic necklaces of jet, except in this case the best surviving examples, which are all of Whitby jet, are known only from find spots in Scotland: the Pitkennedy necklace (Angus), examples from rich graves at Mount Stuart, Bute and Masterton, Fife and substantial fragments from two separate necklaces from another grave at Melfort, Argyll. Even amongst these, one necklace, the one from Mount Stuart, displays many signs of wear, and selective replacement of certain beads. There are a few examples of presumed necklaces which are made up from beads of varying materials and it will be instructive to consider one of these in some detail.

The bead collections from Radwell, Bedfordshire were found with an urn and the cremations of two adults, probably a man and a woman, at the centre of a ring ditch. A total of 120 beads and pendants were recovered. They comprised one complete jet spacer plate, one or more broken spacer plates of amber, one amber pendant, one V-bored amber button, 22 barrel-shaped beads, 9 in amber and 13 in jet, and 94 jet disc beads. As amber pendants do not occur on classic spacer plate necklaces then these items must represent the remains of at least three different necklaces of classic form. The excavators made a valiant attempt to reconstruct a necklace which incorporated all these items, but the result was somewhat curious. Many of the beads were broken and this damage may not all have been caused by modern ploughing. It seems that what we are dealing with is not a necklace as such, but a special collection of carefully gathered heirloom items which might have had uses other than the adornment of the body. Perhaps most of the finds of beads from

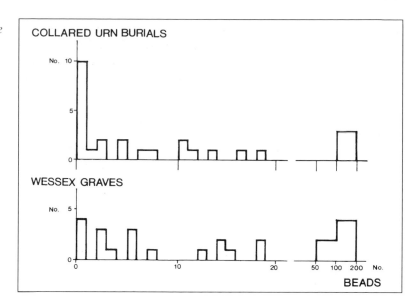

63 *The occurrence of beads with Collared Urns and in Wessex graves.* (author)

barrows were not necklaces at all. In order to investigate this idea further the actual numbers of beads in each barrow burial have been plotted for two main groups of sites, firstly Collared Urn burials which have associated beads and, secondly, the rich Early Bronze Age graves from the Wessex region (**63**). The graphs demonstrate one thing that we have already established — that large collections of beads (over 50 or over 100 items) are extremely rare. The remaining collections of beads all contain less than 20 items and the majority of them (50% or more) occur in groups of less than 8. So we are not talking about actual necklaces, but *remnants* of necklaces. And as most groups contain beads made from several raw materials, as at Radwell, each group probably represents small remnants from several different necklaces. Another interesting aspect of the information presented in the graphs is that, as in the case of the incense cups, the material from the rich Wessex graves and that from the rest of Britain, as represented by beads occurring with Collared Urns, is remarkably similar.

The detailed composition of a 'necklace remnant' can best be illustrated by describing the group of beads and miniature vessel which was excavated to high modern standards by Paul Ashbee within the disc barrow Amesbury G61a located on New Barn Down. The cremated bones of an adult were heaped up in the base of a rectangular pit near the centre of the barrow, and next to this heap a plain incense cup with a double perforation had been placed. Against the cup stood an amber coloured beaver tooth which covered an amber bead. Next to the cup lay a bronze awl, and underneath it a group of beads, one of amber, two of faience, one of red steatite and two cowrie shells. Inside the incense cup was a further amber bead, a fossil bead and two small flint flakes. We may note several interesting points about this deposit. Firstly there are items of many raw materials, all of them exotic: amber, faience, special stone, special bone (the beaver tooth), a fossil and sea shells. Secondly, these items occur in ones and twos only, giving a bead total of ten, and finally, the beads were not deposited in necklace form. The six beads under the cup may have been strung, but another one was placed against the cup and two more inside it. A

117

likely interpretation might be that all these exotic items were not the remains of a piece of feminine jewellery but the special kit belonging to a ritual specialist. This kit comprised pieces of amber which could be rubbed to display magical electrical effects, fossils and shells of fascinating shape from places distant in space and time, beads of rare and piercing blue coloration, and the tooth from a wild animal which could perform miraculous feats of water engineering by building dams with those very teeth. Together with the miniature cup full of aromatic, intoxicating or hallucinogenic substances, and the awl to inscribe signs and patterns on wood, leather or human flesh, such a kit may have been effective in all sorts of medical, religious or divinatory encounters. Rather than being worn as a necklace, or attached to a belt, it seems more likely that the special small items — beads, pendants, amulets and exotic stones and bones — were kept in pouches. Such pouches are thought to have been an important component of dress amongst the communities using Beakers. Some contained fire-making equipment and small flint tools, and may have been fastened by jet or amber buttons. These were generally associated with men. It may be that similar pouches in the Early Bronze Age, fastened by the large V-perforated buttons and which often occur as single items in the graves, were used to protect and hide from general sight the important small groups of exotic items that were the professional equipment of medicine men or shamans. Furthermore, according to the analysis of the bodies and cremated remains recovered from modern excavation of such grave groups, some of these specialists may have been women.

The curious composite nature of the Wessex 'necklaces' has been noted previously by John Barrett. Whilst apparently accepting interpretation of the necklaces in terms of bodily adornment, he does point out that they may have been 'given and worn, split and subdivided,' and were 'indicators of a status bestowed or won from others, the kinds of exchange which created categories of kin, marriage partners, the signs of personal veneration'. The use of beads in such social transactions is well known from anthropological studies around the world, the most famous example undoubtedly being that of the *kula*. The *kula* is an exchange system which has been recorded by social anthropologists amongst the islands to the east of Papua New Guinea (Melanesia) since the pioneering work of Malinowski, published in 1922. Many books have been written concerning the social and political interpretations of the *kula,* but in essence it consists of a double set of person-to-person gift exchanges whereby red spondylus shell necklaces gradually travel from island to island in a clockwise direction, while white shell armbands travel in an anti-clockwise direction. The exchanges involve voyages by canoe, and these voyages, and the exchange ceremonies, are bound up with overt ritual, display and magic. At the same time, barter of a more direct economic nature also takes place. Although many detailed theories of interpretation have been put forward, the general social and economic function of the *kula* is agreed. It is this type of general social context that is probably implied in the words of John Barrett quoted above. Now, I am not suggesting that the people of Early Bronze Age Britain were exchanging segmented faience beads in one direction, in return for amber spacer plates which moved in the other. In fact, although it does seem that the bead types circulated as heirlooms within a social network, the most important aspect of their associations seems to be their probable connection with ritual specialists. However, there are some aspects of the *kula* valuables which may be relevant to the way that we think about the exotic items of the Wessex Early Bronze Age. Firstly, the *kula* necklaces and armbands are ornaments, but are never worn on the human body: they are kept purely as valuables. The items become more valuable and precious with time, and, of course, gradually become more abraded until they completely wear out. Finally, the individual shell items have identities and biographies. Some of the more famous shells have special names, and the history of the life of such a shell through many gift ceremonies will be part of group memory. Perhaps the stories of particular beads, boar's tusk pendants or incense cups were thus recited, or sung, in Early Bronze Age Britain.

Shamanic cults

The idea of prehistoric shamans in Britain is not a new one but has never taken hold in popular imagination. Discussion of shamans and medicine men has ranged from the cautious statement of Colin Burgess that power in Early Bronze Age Wessex may have been held by chiefs who were also priests, or 'divided between chiefs and a class of priests or medicine men', to the more wide-ranging and ambitious theories embraced by Aubrey Burl in his various books on the stone circles and henges of later Neolithic and Bronze Age Britain. As he points out, 'Care has to be taken not to distort the people into copies of ourselves, turning medicine men, shamans or witch doctors into astronomer priests just because the latter fits more comfortably in our modern, technological minds', and he draws attention to the probable importance of fertility magic associated with animals, the use of antlers and horns in ceremonies and various aspects of solar cults, as well as mentioning some of the topics that we have been discussing in this chapter: dancing, chanting, the use of musical instruments such as pipes and drums, and body decoration. But most important of all is Stuart Piggott's other paper on rich Wessex burials.

In addition to his seminal paper of 1938, there is a second paper, relatively little known and called 'From Salisbury Plain to Siberia'. This 1962 publication provides a novel interpretation of the grave group from barrow Upton Lovell G2a that was excavated by Colt Hoare in 1801. The extended skeleton was accompanied by over 60 perforated bone points graded in size, three polished flint axes, two battle axes (one of them broken), various stone rubbers and polishers, perforated boar's tusks and two marcasite cups made by splitting natural nodules from the chalk. The bone points occurred in two main areas, near the feet and on the breast of the skeleton. By comparing these finds with those from a series of burials known from the Baltic Sea to Lake Baikal in Siberia, Piggott was able to suggest that the points had formed fringes sewn onto garments made from skin or fur. Some of the Eurasian graves also contained battle axes, and the graves contained T-shaped bone maces or emblems similar to the T-headed drumsticks which have been used by Lapp and Siberian shamans in the beating of magic drums up to historic times. Other aspects of the Upton Lovell grave goods are also of interest. The two marcasite cups could be special and sparkling versions of the incense cups, the flint axes are archaic heirlooms, originally manufactured in the Neolithic, and many of the stone items were both polished and highly coloured (*see* **61**).

Although barrow Upton Lovell G2a contained the most extensive grave assemblage of this type, other possible graves of shamans are known from Snailwell in Cambridgeshire, where ten graduated perforated bone points and a bone whistle were found with three flint knives, a perforated piece of antler and a Collared Urn, and also from Aldro in Yorkshire, where there were six similar but unperforated points next to the head of the skeleton. There are also two examples from the vicinity of Stonehenge. The first of these, which was noted by Piggott, is the group of animal teeth from the Newton Barrow (South Newton G1). There were sixteen perforated wolves' teeth and two from a dog plus a single globular bead of amber. The other group of objects comes not from a grave, but from the bottom of a 30m deep shaft, located at the centre of a pond barrow (Wilsford G33a: the Wilsford Shaft), which lies a little to the west of Stonehenge in the head of a dry valley. The shaft, possibly a ritual well, may have been dug first in the Neolithic period, and in the Early Bronze Age, the following group of items were dropped into it: eight graduated and perforated bone points similar to those from Snailwell and Upton Lovell, a bone needle, five amber beads, one shale ring and a perforated fossil fish vertebra. It is suggested that all these groups of objects represent the equipment and clothing of shamans, and that most of the other groups or exotic 'Wessex' grave goods represent something very similar. A further hint of probable shamanic activity is provided by a set of four bone tablets found in a barrow in the Lake group near Stonehenge. One is plain, but the others bear lightly engraved patterns of stars and crosses which appear in reverse on the under sides. When William Cunnington first saw them he thought that they could have been used in casting lots — for telling fortunes or foretelling the future. Strangely enough, from a barrow at Folkton in Yorkshire, an almost exactly similar set of geometric engravings was found on a series of four bone beads. The grave also contained a clay Food Vessel, some pig bones, a bronze awl and a flint scraper, and, as this barrow was excavated by Canon Greenwell, the bones were properly studied and we know that the adult person interred in the grave was a woman.

Returning to the set of 'Wessex' grave groups that was defined originally by Piggott, it can be proposed that there are three different types of grave represented. The first and largest group includes the sets of shamanic equipment that we have been discussing: the remnants of necklaces made from exotic magical substances, complex multi-coloured pendants, items of gold, polished stone palettes and special miniature vessels of stone or clay which were designed for the burning of 'peculiar substances'. Amongst this group, there is a subgroup of grave assemblages which are dominated by objects made from polished stone, bone and teeth, and this subgroup includes, of course, the shaman's grave from Upton Lovell. The second group of burials contains metal items in association with objects of polished bone or stone. There are two subgroups — one has daggers and bone objects, the other pins or axes and other objects mainly of stone. There are no miniature vessels and no exotic beads. The significance of these associations is not immediately apparent at present and further work is needed. The third and final group consists of just a few graves that stand out as being very rich. Included here are the burial in Wilsford G23 with daggers, a pin and a series of objects in stone and bone (one of them the swan bone whistle) and Bush Barrow itself (Wilsford G5). Thus, this rich assemblage with its daggers, axe, pieces of goldwork and exotic items of stone and bone, which has been taken as the typical example of a Wessex chieftain's grave, can now be seen to be quite different from the general repertoire of Wessex burials. As so few modern identifications of sex and

64 *Types of grave goods found with Collared Urns. (Figures, taken from Longworth 1984, denote numbers of graves, not numbers of items)*

Weapons and tools

bronze dagger	bronze knife or razor	bronze awl	bone dagger pommel	flint arrowhead	flint knife	stone macehead or battle-axe	whetstone
3	26	41	9	26	43	17	8

Bodily adornment and beads

bone pin	bone belt hook	clay ear plug	clay or calcite bead	bone bead or pendant	gold or bronze bead	amber bead	faience bead	jet bead
46	2	3	5	14	5	20	12	44

Special items

accessory cup	bone tweezers	boar tusk	wolf tooth	fossil	shell	white quartz	rock crystal
76	2	3	1	4	2	2	1

age have been possible from the human remains found in the graves, it cannot be said to what extent any of these types of grave good were buried with men, women or children. Indeed, even the sex of Hoare's 'tall and stout man' from Bush Barrow cannot be checked because the bones were not retained.

Having established that the majority of the rich graves in Wessex contained ritual equipment and not the regalia of chieftains and their consorts, it is worth looking at the general tenor of Early Bronze Age grave groups found outside Wessex. As in previous analyses in this chapter we shall use the goods found with Collared Urns as a representative sample. In figure **64** these grave goods have been grouped into three categories: weapons and tools, bodily adornment and beads, and special items. All the types of grave good listed in the table are similar to those found in the rich graves of Wessex, and there are very few items from the Wessex graves that do not occur also with Collared Urns. Such items are the highly exotic pieces such as the more elaborate goldwork, composite pendants and bronze axes. Otherwise, daggers, knives and awls occur widely in both series of graves, as do stone battle axes, bone pins, accessory cups, and beads made from a wide range of exotic substances. Of particular interest are the occurrences of the special items, listed in figure **64**. As well as the accessory cups these include some of the very things that we have drawn attention to in the Wessex graves: special shiny stones, fossils, animal teeth and shells. In fact, the ranges of items found in graves throughout Britain can be used to argue that the sets of ritual equipment — mainly beads of magical composition, miniature vessels and special objects selected from nature — may have belonged to specialist medicine men or shamans who practised their important rites and ceremonies throughout the country. The only thing that is really different about Wessex is that there is a distinct concentration of such graves around Stonehenge, near Avebury, on Cranborne Chase, and in the Wylye valley. And that may be due to a particular historical process, whereby the practitioners of a cult which was fast becoming obsolete, or their followers, chose to bury them in the areas of their ancient ancestral monuments.

Thus the concentration of burials of ritual equipment in Wiltshire may represent the final deposition of the most precious possessions of the last practising shamans of this particular cult. The already outmoded habit of the ritual burning and inhalation of exotic substances may have at last given way to the alternative delights of alcohol just as, at the same time, the traditional mobile way of life gradually became supplanted by the ordered habitation of permanent farmsteads and fields. Life would never be the same again.

Notes

A catalogue of wristguards from Beaker graves, to 1970, is in Clarke 1970, page 438. For the one from Barnack: Kinnes in Donaldson 1977.

The classic paper on the Wessex Culture is Piggott 1938. There are no recent general summaries of the material and its interpretation, but useful guides to the objects and raw materials can be found in Clarke et al 1985 and the Devizes Museum Catalogue: Annable and Simpson 1964. For Mike Parker Pearson's comments, see Parker Pearson 1999, 89. Grinsell 1974 provides a summary of disc barrows and their contents. A full appreciation of the range of graves is best gained by reading the original accounts in Colt Hoare 1812 and 1821.

Grahame Clark's book on exotic substances is Clark 1986. For psychoactive substances, see Sherratt 1991 and 1995. The statistics relating to finds associated with Collared Urns have been compiled using Longworth 1984.

For illustrations of amber necklaces see Clarke et al 1985, plates 4.29 and 4.51; for the Scottish jet necklaces: plates 4.90, 5.45, 5.48 and 5.50. The Radwell (Felmersham) beads are described and illustrated in Hall and Woodward 1977. For Amesbury G61a see Ashbee 1984, figures 12, 13, 38 and 39.

The quotation from John Barrett concerning necklaces is from Barrett 1994, 122; for the *kula* system see Malinowski 1922 and Leach and Leach 1983. The shamanic ideas quoted are from Burgess 1980, 175, Burl 1976, 86-7 and Burl 1979, 202-214. The paper on the shaman's grave from Upton Lovell G2a by Piggott is Piggott 1962. The Wilsford Shaft items are illustrated in Ashbee et al 1989, figures 43-46. The carved bone tablets from Lake are illustrated in Burl 1979, figure 92; the bone beads from Folkton in Kinnes and Longworth 1985, 79, Burial 6.

6   Barrows in a sensory world

Recent interest in the phenomenology of archaeological landscapes has been inspired by the writings of philosophers such as Merleau-Ponty and Heidegger. Phenomenology concerns the ways in which humans experience and interpret the world around them. In landscape terms, such studies revolve around the concepts of place and space. In essence, the study of place concerns the analysis of sites and locations as static positions, where human actions are carried out. On the other hand, the concept of space implies the movement of bodies, animals and things between places and across landscapes. Such movements, in the human world, relate closely to patterns of tracks and pathways. Anthropological studies in many different parts of the world have shown that people experience landscape in several important ways. Many aspects of spaces and places are interpreted as symbols in the human mind. The patterns of symbolism are linked into an appreciation of ancestral powers: memorised biographies and genealogies of people, places and supernatural spirits that reach far back into the mythological past. The perceived links to time past and spiritual 'other' worlds are consolidated by traditional stories and songs, and the unique character of individual locations are embedded through creative methods of place-naming. Readers will recognise that approaches such as these have already been used in many parts of this book. But so far they have been applied at the site or artefact level. For instance, we have considered the importance of the repeated rebuilding of structures and mounds on spots that already were imbued with ancient ancestral powers, or looked at grave goods in terms of how their colour and texture might have been perceived by the human senses. In this chapter, such themes will be extended to the analysis of landscape spaces, and the barrows contained within them.

Attempting to apply phenomenological ideas to some archaeological evidence from Britain, Chris Tilley undertook studies of the locations of tombs and barrows in southern Wales and on Cranborne Chase. In the Black Mountains region of south-east Wales, he identified four Cotswold-Severn chambered long cairns which were aligned on the courses of local rivers, and nine whose alignments appeared to have been orientated on major hilltops visible along the western escarpment of the Black Mountains. He concluded that in this way, 'the monuments draw out and emphasise important features of the landscape: the axes of the river valleys and prominent spurs, paths of movement and prominent landmarks whose ancestral significance had already been established during the Mesolithic . . .'. It is noticeable that the major advances in archaeological thought often attract rapid and wide-ranging controversy. In this case, the study of the Black Mountains long cairns has been closely criticised by Andrew Fleming. Following a process of checking on the ground, he pointed out that many of the proposed alignments are not at all precise, that the numbers of sites considered are too few, and that several other types of idea can be advanced to explain the local placing and orientation of individual tombs. Such criticism is constructive in that it tends to stimulate a more rigorous style of analysis for such sets of evidence. It does not disqualify the general approach. One way to move forward within such lines of inquiry is to work with larger numbers of sites, and to check theoretical patterns of visibility and intervisibility using mathematical means. This can be achieved by employing GIS computer applications and this method has been used successfully in the extensive studies of barrows in Wiltshire and Dorset. The results of some of these studies will be drawn upon later in this chapter.

Tomb, tor and cave

One of the key results of the Bodmin Moor survey was the appreciation of the huge variety of barrow and cairn constructions that had been employed in prehistoric times. Some of the many types and sizes of cairn were illustrated in chapter 1; here particular attention will be drawn to those types located upon the natural rock outcrops known as tors, and those which incorporated small tors at their centres, or which had been built up around single earthfast boulders called grounders (*see* **6**: 25, 30 and 36). Chris Tilley has emphasised that the incorporation of these natural features involved the controlling of significant natural features by making them part of human ritual activities. Thus the tor became the cairn, but the cairn still represented the tor. It was a kind of domestication or humanisation of key landscape foci. In the area around Leskernick Hill it was only selected tors or grounders that were treated in this way during the Bronze Age. And those selected tended to be those which had already been incorporated into hilltop enclosures during the Neolithic period, or those which were located close to such enclosures. These also tended to include the tors with the most dramatic profiles, such as those on Rough Tor, or the Cheesewring at Stowe's Pound. Spread widely across Cornwall there are also a series of simple stone chamber tombs, or dolmens, locally known by the name 'Quoit'. These may never have been totally covered by stone cairns or earth mounds and appear to have been built to mimic the natural stone formations of the local granite tors. Chris Tilley had also noticed a similar set of relationships amongst the dolmens of south-west Wales. In the area of north Pembrokeshire, the dolmens seem to be located close to dramatic natural outcrops of rock, or in specific locations such that more distant outcrops of particular significance are clearly in view (**colour plate 23, 24**). However Richard Bradley has pointed out that such megalithic tombs also occur in areas where no such natural stone outcrops occur. He argues that people in prehistory may not have perceived the difference between natural features and built monuments in the same way that we do. They may have interpreted the natural outcrops as ruined tombs, and therefore included them as ancestral relics in their Neolithic hilltop enclosures or, later on, inside their round cairns of stone or earth.

Connections such as those we have just discussed are of a fairly wide-ranging general nature. Sometimes it is possible to detect close and specific symbolic relations between a natural feature and a single monument. At Parc le Broes Cwm on the Gower peninsula in south Wales there is a chambered long cairn of Cotswold-Severn type; it was excavated in 1869, and again by Richard Atkinson in 1960 and 1961. The tomb is unusually sited in a hidden location on the floor of a narrow dry valley. Also in the valley, there are two limestone caves, one of which is visible from the tomb. These caves are known to have been used by people at times within the Palaeolithic, Mesolithic, Beaker and Early Bronze Age periods. Amongst the human bones and other items found within the tomb there were some animal bones which produced very early pre-Neolithic radiocarbon dates and some pieces of stalactite and quartz. Alasdair Whittle argued that these items may have come from the caves. The caves may have been connected by the Neolithic community with the ancestral past, and the tomb may have been built in this valley for that very reason. Thus the tomb echoed the role and form of the cave, while the cave may have been viewed as an ancestral tomb-like place. Certainly, some of the human and animal bones from the tomb had calcareous deposits on them, and these may have been taken from earlier burials previously interred in one of the caves.

Hills and hollows

Near the highest section of the South Dorset Ridgeway lies a particular concentration of barrows along Bronkham Hill. The barrows mainly sit on the crest of the ridge, but the ridge itself is very undulating, so that as one walks along barrows tend to come in and out of view. Amongst the barrows, and on either flank of the ridge, are many sink holes or dolines (**colour plate 25**). These are circular, deep holes, on average 8m in diameter, formed naturally by sinkage into hollows formed by underground solution of the chalk below the acid surface deposits of gravel and sand. Although geologists have argued that the dolines here date mainly from recent times, there is evidence to suggest that some of them were present much earlier. Chris Tilley has argued that the concentration of barrows on Bronkham Hill was directly related to the presence of the dolines. Indeed, the hollows may have provided loose gravel and soil for their construction. As Tilley states: 'One is a transformation or inversion of the other'. Both the hollows and the barrow mounds are circular, and the upturned bowl shape of the mounds is a direct reflection of the curvaceous and dished profile of the dolines. 'It is not hard to imagine that during the Bronze Age these circular sink holes were conceptualised as sites of ancestral activity: the places where ancestors entered and exited into the land to a sea of the underworld existing below . . . The dolines formed an essential part of the mystery and power of the place.' There are other concentrations of sink holes known on the Dorset heathlands, and some of these, such as those on Bryants Puddle Heath, are again associated with round barrows. There are also sink holes in the valley where the Poor Lot barrow cemetery is situated (**65**). And some of the sink holes lie in significant gaps within the alignment of small barrows that lies at right angles to the northern row (*see* **46**). It seems unlikely that such holes were formed after the construction of the barrows, and so they may have been incorporated into the overall scheme of the cemetery as a deliberate and highly symbolic act. Something rather similar was taking place on the Yorkshire Wolds. Terry Manby noticed that some pits containing deposits of later Neolithic pottery on the ridge east of Rudston Beacon may originally have been natural sink holes. These may have been dug out to obtain the useful clay filling and then filled with special selections of decorated pottery and fine flintwork. Bronze Age barrows again lie nearby. Many of the barrows excavated by Mortimer on the Wold tops contained thick layers of clay and flint, and this may well have been dug out from nearby dolines. At Vessey Ponds, hollows that still hold water were associated with scatters of flintwork of Mesolithic,

65 *Bell barrow and sink hole in the Poor Lot barrow cemetery.* (Peter Woodward)

Neolithic and Bronze Age date. No barrows lie directly adjacent to the ponds, but there are several in the near vicinity.

On a much larger scale it can be observed that certain barrows appear to represent in miniature the actual hills upon which they sit, or the profiles of hills visible directly from them. Hambledon Hill in north Dorset is an isolated and steep sided eminence, dominated by a large Iron Age hillfort and the early Neolithic causewayed enclosure: Roger Mercer's 'gigantic necropolis constructed for the exposure of the cadaveric remains of a large population' (**colour plate 26**). There are two long barrows on the hill. One of them is directly associated with the structure and functions of the causewayed enclosure and has been excavated. The other is a massively substantial mound which lies away from the Neolithic camp and inside the later hillfort. It lies directly along the spine of the north segment of the hill and appears to be a smaller version of the ridge itself — both when viewed from below, and when walking along the top of the hill. Another example of a similar optical effect is found in north Wiltshire. The Giants Grave long barrow, in the parish of Milton Lilbourne, sits on the very edge of Salisbury Plain above a deep and steep re-entrant of the chalk escarpment. Looking across the narrow Vale of Pewsey one's gaze hits the outline of a significant hill with a dramatic whale-backed profile. This is Martinsell Hill, surmounted by two Iron Age enclosures and, no doubt, the site of many earlier activities. Standing next to the Giants Grave, the outline of the barrow appears as a miniature version of Martinsell which looms behind it. At short distances to the north-east or south-west along the scarp this visual effect cannot be achieved, and the siting of the barrow in this particular spot appears to have been quite deliberate.

The circle of life

For many years I have been studying the internal arrangements of barrow cemeteries in Wessex, and gathering information on the dateable grave goods found within the mounds which have been excavated. In the south Dorset region Peter Woodward noticed that the richest Early Bronze Age burials were clustered not on the Ridgeway, as had previously been emphasised, but in some mainly destroyed barrows which occurred close to the henges and other monuments near the River Frome, and within another arc of barrows built on a set of lower ridges between the Ridgeway and the river. Thus the barrows appeared to be arranged in a series of nested arcs. These arcs were closely related to the local topography and centred on the important ceremonial monuments around Dorchester. In the light of this observation, we began to study the configurations of round barrows around the two main ceremonial centres in Wiltshire, near Avebury and around Stonehenge. Although the barrow locations in both regions were heavily influenced by the scale and nature of the local topography, in both cases it became apparent that the barrows lay on theoretical arcs or circles, centring on the major monuments themselves. We suggested that these curvilinear settings of barrows may have been symbolic in function, defining a finite area of space imbued with ritual meaning. They may have formed a powerful boundary beyond which few people were allowed to pass. At Stonehenge, the pattern is particularly marked with two concentric circles of barrows focused on the circular stone monument itself. This idea has been adapted and developed by Mike Parker Pearson in his consideration of Stonehenge as a monument of death. He views the dense inner circle of barrows as defining a distinct domain of the ancestors and the area between the inner and outer circles as a transitional zone where Early Bronze Age burials were more diffusely distributed. Thus Stonehenge was a central focus within a concentrically arranged monumental landscape.

I also suggested that these circular patterns might indicate that in the Early Bronze Age there may have been an underlying symbolic principle, based on the concept of the circle, which operated at a series of levels — in monument building, funerary activity and the placing of visible structures in the landscape. Thus the large scale patterns of circular settings and arcs of mounds reflect the shape of the round barrows contained within them, the stake and post rings which lie beneath some of them, and the shape of the timber and stone monuments upon which they focus.

This idea of the circle as a symbol has now been discussed in exciting detail by Richard Bradley in his book *The Significance of Monuments*. He contends that the circular monuments of Late Neolithic and Early Bronze Age Britain and Ireland 'can be understood as interpretations of a circular archetype which reflects a more general perception of the world'. The development of circular monuments led to a greater involvement of larger numbers of people within ceremonies that took place within them. Some, like the banked henges, produced concealed ritual space, while open stone circles could be related visually to other monuments, and barrows, in the landscapes around them. One of the most fascinating aspects of Bradley's book is the picture he selected for the cover. This is a circular photomontage of the views out, in every direction, from the centre of a stone circle towards the distant horizons. The composite image provides a striking rendition of the human experience of looking out into landscapes. Another similar approach involves the production of computer stitched animated panoramas compiled from overlapping photographs. This technique has been employed in the University of Birmingham barrows project which will be mentioned later. Both pictorial processes attempt to demonstrate the way that people experience their surroundings in terms of a circular impression of the world that can be sensed by the human body. Such sensual impressions are not however limited to visual effects.

Sensory archaeology

In the western world, we are familiar with a five-fold division of the human senses. The five are taste, touch, smell, hearing and vision. In western thought, vision and sight are in fact held to be much more significant than the other senses. In other cultures, the senses may be classified in different ways, and in many of them, hearing and smell may be of greater general significance than sight. But, however they may be conceptualised, the human senses form a strong system of categories of perception through which aspects of the world around can be valued and interpreted. Much of this chapter does concentrate on the examination of the role of the visual sense in relation to barrows, but in this section we shall extend this approach to consider colour, and also mention some aspects of touch and sound.

The deliberate selection of white rocks, especially luminous quartz, for incorporation in Neolithic and Bronze Age monuments has been discussed by Frances Lynch, and readers will recall the fragments of quartz built into the cairn at Brenig 51 (page 83). At Knowth, in the Boyne valley of eastern Ireland, the facing wall included white quartz, black granodiorite, and siltstone cobbles which display blue and white stripes. In the Clava cairns of north-east Scotland, red sandstone blocks are positioned to catch the rays of light from the setting sun, while grey and white slabs are placed so that they are lit up by the rising sun. Thus the cool grey stones symbolise the brightness of dawn, while the warm sandstone blocks reflect the ruddy sunset glow. The work of Andrew Jones on Arran has shown a three-fold symbolism, with the use of red and white stones, alongside blades and flakes made from black pitchstone, in the Clyde tombs. Red sandstone from the fertile coastal plain seems to represent softness, flesh and blood, and fertility; white rocks from the northern mountains refer to light and the whiteness of bones; and the black pitchstone symbolises darkness and death. Jones argues that the symbolism of the colours of the stones is more important than their aesthetic effect. Certainly many of the red and white stones occur deep inside the chambers where little natural light penetrated.

Meanwhile, work in northern Scotland has shown that some Neolithic tombs appear to have been designed and built so that some very specific auditory effects might have been achieved. The production of sound in the form of singing, chanting or, most probably, drumming, within the enclosed chambers could have led to distinctive noise levels, with eerie echo effects. Frighteningly loud within the chamber, little sound would have penetrated to any people gathered outside the tomb. Scientific experiments carried out by Aaron Watson have further shown that at some tombs, such as Camster Round in Caithness, drumming could have set up resonance within the tomb. Although the sounds produced would have been too low for humans to hear, the resonance may have been picked up physically as deep vibrations.

66 *The long barrow in the Lake group near Stonehenge today lies in a wood. Long barrows also may have been situated in forest during the Neolithic, or have been covered by regenerated woodland at later times in prehistory.* (© Crown copyright. NMR)

The key to achieving a multi-sensory interpretation of barrows is to place one's own human body amongst them. By walking in, over and around a barrow or tomb, and by exploring every corner of a barrow cemetery at different times of day, during the changing seasons of the year and under varying weather conditions, a twenty-first-century person can begin to appreciate the feel of the place and of the monuments. The sort of feelings that can be evoked include aspects of what can be seen, both in the near and distant fields of view, colours and textures, noise levels and echoes, optical effects and odours, and the impact of sun, rain or mist. And more general sensory impressions can also be perceived. Two extreme examples are the closed-in effect caused by tomb chambers or tightly-bounded valley bottom or hollow locations, and the open 'top of the world' effect experienced on certain hilltops and platform barrows. The former feelings may be safe and womb-like or, alternatively, claustrophobic and full of foreboding, while the high locations may provoke feelings of airy euphoria or agoraphobic panic. Different people may experience different effects and it is often instructive to walk sites in the company of others — different sensory perceptions may be shared, and the effects of group consciousness explored.

Such an approach has been developed over the last four years by a small team studying the barrows around Stonehenge and in south Dorset, and some of the results will shortly be described. But before that, brief reference will be made to another survey with related aims, which was carried out by Shannon Fraser in Ireland. In an analysis of the Neolithic passage tomb cemetery of Loughcrew, she focused attention on the open spaces between and around the tombs. These spaces were perceived to have provided arenas where large public groups may have gathered to witness the hidden rites that were being enacted secretly inside the tombs. The tombs occupy the four summits of a distinctive range of hills. The flat summits are reached by scaling steep slopes and form hidden 'interior worlds' which appear quite suddenly as the final change of slope is negotiated. On Carnbane East the edges of two adjoining level summit areas, and breaks of slope within them, have been emphasised by the apparently careful placing of the cairn monuments, and the largest tomb is sited such that the passage entrance opens onto a small natural platform. On Carnbane West the summit comprises a set of adjacent level areas which are screened from each other by a series of natural knolls and ridges. Again, the margins of these areas, and the passageways between them, were marked out and enhanced by the placement of the tombs. Thus movements within and between the visually enclosed spaces were strictly prescribed and controlled.

We have seen that the work of Chris Tilley has highlighted the importance of attempting to understand the detailed landscape setting of barrows. This involves looking at how barrows relate to natural features, the quality of the views from them, and the lines of visibility between them. However his approach is hampered by the problems caused by modern land use, especially the tracts of woodland which in the present day rural landscape impede many of the view lines that require analysis (**66**). By using computer techniques it is possible to overcome this difficulty, as it is a relatively simple task to calculate and map the areas that are visible from any one site. The total area visible (visarea) and this area as seen on a map related to the Ordnance Survey grid (viewshed) can be computed using standard GIS packages, and potential patterns can be statistically analysed. Such theoretical research does of course need to be accompanied by programmes of systematic fieldwork, preferably over different seasons and in varying weather conditions, designed to check view lines which are not today obscured by trees. At the same time the detailed landscape settings of monuments may be assessed, and records of the topographical aspect and atmospheric 'feel' of the sites made. Taking all these points and processes into account, a major project designed to study the locations of long and round barrows was initiated at the University of Birmingham in 1994. Such intricate and wide ranging analysis cannot be attempted by a single person and in this case the project has involved the skills of four researchers, two of them computer analysts with archaeological interests, and two archaeologists, one of whom possesses wide experience of computer applications. These are my friends and colleagues Sally Exon, Vince Gaffney and Ron Yorston. The main topic of study has been 1,200 barrows and other monuments in the area around Stonehenge, and the results of this work are to be published shortly as a book in association with a computer disk. The book will present an analysis of the development of the Stonehenge landscape from the Mesolithic through to the Early Bronze Age. This will be one possible reading of the mass of visual and animated data, and circular panoramas, which will be available on the disk for other researchers to explore on their own computer screens. The images in **colour plates 26** and **27** provide a static

67 *Aerial view from Normanton Down to Lake.* (© Crown copyright. NMR)

preview of some of the sorts of data that will be available: the viewshed of a major long barrow, showing which other earlier Neolithic sites were in view, and the area of view from the Stonehenge Avenue where it crosses the King Barrow Ridge. This shows the pattern of barrows of all types, long and round, as well as ploughed sites surviving only as ring ditches, and of henge monuments, which can be seen from this viewpoint. The project also involved an assessment of the degree to which the theoretical areas of view might have been influenced by the vegetation that is thought to have been present during the different time periods.

One aspect of the project concentrated on a detailed study of the spatial arrangements of the main barrow cemeteries in the vicinity of Stonehenge, and an analysis of how views and sight lines varied as one walked along the rows of barrows and amongst them. The recurring pattern of small clusters, and the nature of the dateable grave groups found within them, has already been described for one of the cemeteries: that on Normanton Down (*see* chapter 5, **56**). The view out from Stonehenge towards this large and roughly linear group is very familiar. However, the barrows are actually more striking when viewed from the 'back', in other words from the south. The air photograph figure **67** shows a vista to the south. The Normanton Down barrows are in the centre of the image; beyond is the dry valley which runs east from Wilsford Down and the ridge where the Wilsford and Lake barrow groups are situated. The Lake group lies mainly in the triangular wood near the top right-hand corner of the picture. Views of the Normanton barrows from the south — both from the ridge and from the bottom of the dry valley — may have been important in various ways at different times in prehistory, and it is aspects such as this which will be considered in detail in the book resulting from the Birmingham barrows project. Here we shall concentrate on the study of changing degrees of visibility along and within single cemeteries and this will be illustrated by an investigation of sight patterns amongst the Cursus barrow group (**68**).

This cemetery falls into six small clusters and these can be seen to form two main groups, at west and east, each of nine barrows (five plus two plus two in the west and six plus three in the east), with a small cluster of three barrows between them. According to the occurrence of Beaker burials the western of the two clusters may have been earlier than the eastern group, which consists of the row of prominent bell barrows. The western cluster congregates around the Fargo Plantation mini henge and contains only one fancy barrow. An alternative reading of the spatial pattern is that there were two main barrow rows on different alignments — one marked by the four Beaker barrows and the other the run of closely spaced bell barrows. Again a basic west and east division is apparent. The probably earlier western group is out of view of Stonehenge but commands good sight lines to many of the existing Neolithic monuments of the area, including several long barrows. Also of course it is spatially related to the western end of the Stonehenge Cursus. From the eastern group of fancy barrows some of these earlier sites are still in sight but the views are dominated by the site of Stonehenge which looms in the centre ground to the south. Thus it can be perceived that the placing of the barrows in relation to what could be seen changed through time in an interesting and systematic way.

A barrow with a view: the long barrows of south Dorset

To complement the work around Stonehenge, a more modest project was designed to study the visual settings of the long barrows, Neolithic monuments and selected round barrows in south Dorset. For this a series of viewshed plots was generated by Sally Exon and the fieldwork and research were carried out by my husband and myself.

Data relating to 20 long barrows and various other monuments of Late Neolithic and Early Bronze Age date along and around the South Dorset Ridgeway were analysed. Very few of the long barrows have been excavated and even fewer have provided material suitable for radiocarbon dating. The Maiden Castle bank barrow was constructed by 3350 BC. Although quite extensively excavated by Sir Mortimer Wheeler and in the campaign of the 1980s, no evidence of burials was recovered. The monument at Alington Avenue was totally excavated but had previously been ploughed flat, and the only finds were flintwork and an ox skull. Otherwise only one barrow was excavated by an antiquarian who left a record of the investigation. The barrow at Forty Acre Plantation, Bradford Peverell was opened by Edward Cunnington in 1881 and in a cairn at the south-east end he found a small fragment of human jaw, two pieces of pottery and a flint implement.

68 *The Cursus group: barrow types and burial contents.* (©: Exon, Gaffney, Woodward and Yorston)

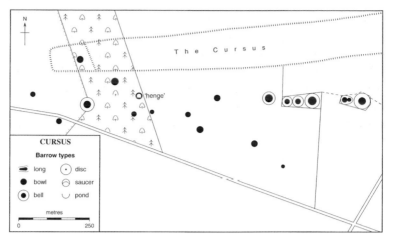

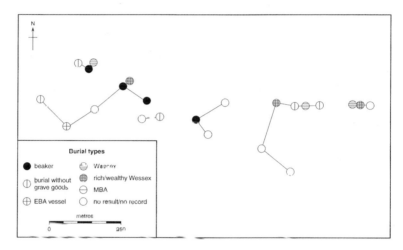

Near the other end, and higher in the mound, was a crouched skeleton. Most of the barrows seem to have been of earth construction, but two are known to have contained chambers of stone. At Hell Stone, Portesham, only the chamber, with its stones much re-arranged, survives, but the Grey Mare with Her Colts retains more of the original structure (**69**). There are remains of a mound of tapering outline; this may have been surrounded by a revetment of stone slabs. The stone chamber occupies the south-east end and there may also have been a crescent-shaped forecourt in front of it. The chamber was opened in the early nineteenth century, when some pottery and many human bones were discovered. The local monuments that were probably contemporary with the extended use of the various long barrows are the causewayed enclosure at Maiden Castle, a related enclosure at Flagstones, the henges of Maumbury, Dorchester and Mount Pleasant, and four stone circles at Kingston Russell, Hampton, Little Mayne and The Nine Stones.

The results of the computer analysis of degrees of visibility between the long barrows are summarised in figure **70**. The levels of visual connectedness between sites can best be considered by dividing the viewlines into those of short, medium and longer lengths.

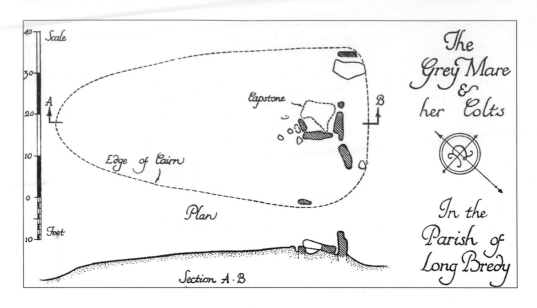

69 *The Grey Mare and her Colts, Dorset.* (© Crown copyright. NMR)

Starting with the short viewlines of less than 2.5km, four localised groups of intervisible barrows emerge (**70**, A). The most dispersed is the western group ranged around the upper reaches of the valley of the South Winterborne river and the west end of the Ridgeway at Martin's Down; these are also related visually to the sites of three stone circles. Further east there are three tightly spaced clusters — one on the east end of the Ridgeway at Culliford Tree, one on the ridge between the valleys of the South Winterborne and the Frome rivers, and the last in the vicinity of the Neolithic causewayed enclosure at Maiden Castle. All three of these eastern groups are closely knitted in by sight-lines to the Neolithic sites around Dorchester. Two long barrows to the south-west do not appear to fit into such a spatial pattern. These are the two sites with stone chambers and they will be considered further at a later stage in this account. Of the small clusters displayed in figure **70**, three are closely linked to river systems — one at the headwaters of the South Winterborne, the second perched on the south side of the Frome valley and a third, Culliford Tree, at the head of a dry valleys which run down to Little Mayne, adjacent to the source of a tributary of the River Frome. The knoll at Maiden Castle also overlooks the South Winterborne to the south, but all the long barrows here appear to face north. This general pattern of close relations between small long barrow clusters and river sources had also been noted around Stonehenge.

When longer view lines, those 2.5-5km (1.5-3 miles), are taken into account, a second and more simple picture emerges (**70**, B). There are two main groups visible, one in the west and one in the east. The western group is strongly linked in visual terms to the bank barrow on Martin's Down (**71**), but in the eastern group every single long barrow is intervisible with the Maiden Castle bank barrow. Also the lines of orientation of most of them point in the direction of Maiden Castle. Another key monument that seems to link

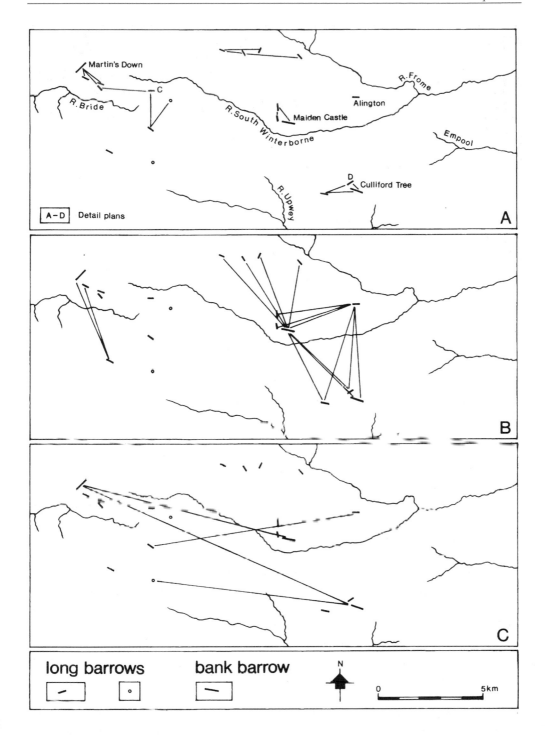

70 *Lines of view between the long barrows of south Dorset: A. less than 2.5 km; B. 2.5 to 5 km; C. over 5 km. (Ann and Peter Woodward)*

in the three localised groups of the eastern sector is that excavated at Alington Avenue. Viewlines verified by the GIS analysis that were over 5km in length (**70**, C) show that the two ends of the Ridgeway, and the western and eastern groups in general were intervisible in theory. However, these long-distance links could not be achieved by human eye during fieldwork.

It could be argued that many of the theoretical view-lines discussed above may have been masked or obscured by woodland in the Neolithic period. However, if the monuments had been highlighted by white chalk capping or pinpointed by smoke from fires and beacons the view lines could still have been highly significant. Perhaps people travelled in from distant places to a specific ancestral monument, and remained there awhile before progressing by traditionally prescribed pathways and natural markers to the large enclosure at Maiden Castle. Suggestions that extensive ceremonial activities took place at the various long barrows have been gained from detailed field evaluation of the individual sites. Firstly, as alluded to above, all the barrows are related, in terms of topographical and visual orientation, to the major inland streams and rivers. Secondly, most of them are sited such that they are just below the summit of local ridges and spurs. This means that the view out is blocked in one particular direction, and that direction is usually to the south or south-west. Finally, in quite a few cases the barrows were sited so that there was a large naturally occurring level platform just in front of, or to one side of, the mound. To illustrate these points, details of a selection of four sites, taken from the full project archive, will be presented here.

At Forty Acre Plantation, the long barrow is sited on a spur between two dry re-entrants of the Frome valley (**72**, A). The mound is aligned on the direction of river flow and it commands long views up the valley towards the headwaters and, from the higher end of the mound, downstream in the direction of Flagstones and the great henge enclosure of Mount Pleasant. To the south a fine far view of the Ridgeway can be obtained although sight of Maiden Castle is today obscured by trees. But to the south-west, the rising spur forms a close horizon. The long barrow at Red Barn (**72**, B) again occupies a spur between dry side valleys of the River Frome. Fine far-reaching views up the main valley are again in evidence, and also, as at Forty Acre Plantation, there is a close horizon to the south-west. The orientation of the mound, and the location of the higher end, do not reflect the flow line of the river, but the direction of view towards Maiden Castle, and the area immediately west of the mound could have provided a large level platform. The Longlands long barrow, now ploughed out, is aligned along the South Winterborne, and is sited on the south slope of the valley (**72**, C). To the south and south-west the view is obscured by the rising hillside. Much today is blocked by trees but, looking up the narrow valley, the source of the Winterborne near Martin's Down could probably have been seen, and downstream, GIS data confirmed that the spot later occupied by the Nine Stones circle would have been clearly visible. Furthermore the axis of the mound points straight at it. At Culliford Tree, the Whitcombe long barrow lies at an angle on a north-facing spur between the heads of two dry valleys (**72**, D). These run down to a zone above the present day Empool, a tributary of the River Frome, a zone which still retains a few large sarsen stones. These are the remnants of a larger spread which may have been in part the remains of a prehistoric stone circle. The higher end of the barrow points directly down the eastern

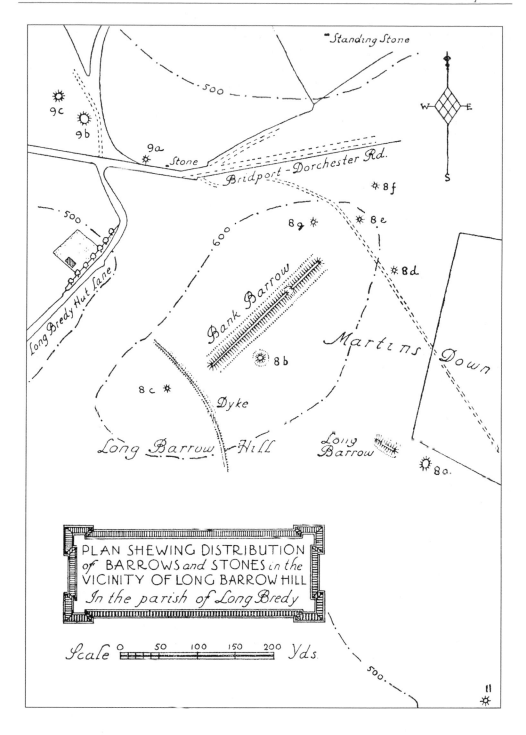

71 *Martin's Down, Dorset. (© Crown copyright. NMR)*

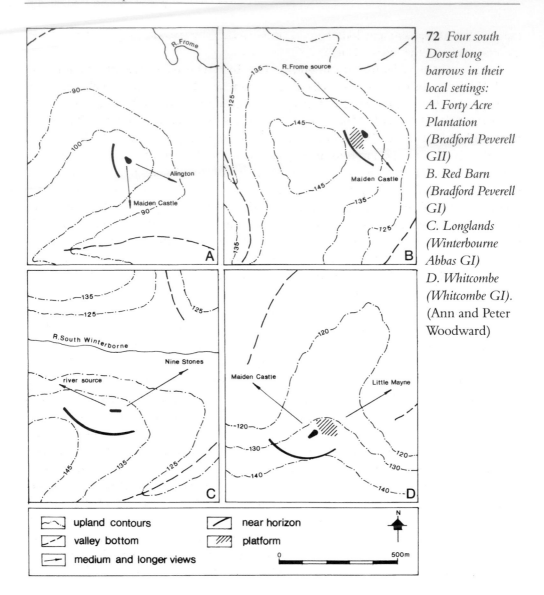

72 *Four south Dorset long barrows in their local settings: A. Forty Acre Plantation (Bradford Peverell GII) B. Red Barn (Bradford Peverell GI) C. Longlands (Winterbourne Abbas GI) D. Whitcombe (Whitcombe GI). (Ann and Peter Woodward)*

of the two valleys towards the site of this stone monument at Little Mayne. As in many of the other cases considered, the view to the south is blocked by a near horizon and there is a distinct level platform visible in front of the higher end of the barrow.

From these field studies, and those of other long barrows in the south Dorset group, it has been noted that in many cases there are level platforms in front of, or next to, the mound. These platforms were probably natural in origin but their profiles may have been enhanced during the process of mound construction. If designed for the enactment of periodic festivals and rituals then these ceremonies may have been connected to the movements of sun or moon. The blocked horizons occurring on the south and south-west sides of the barrows may have been related to the setting of the sun at midwinter, and it is interesting to note that it is this very phenomenon that is thought to have influenced the siting of the prominent long barrow on Gussage Cow Down, which later became incorporated into the Dorset Cursus.

It remains to consider the class of unusual long barrows that are especially common in south Dorset — the bank barrows. The massive example at Broadmayne, which marks the eastern end of the South Dorset Ridgeway, commands similar views down the dry valley towards the site of the Little Mayne stone circle as were experienced from the Whitcombe barrow, illustrated above (**72**, D). However, the monument is placed on the high ridge top such that the direct view south to the sea and the Isle of Portland are also dominant. At Martin's Down (**71**) the bank barrow is clearly of two phases. The original long barrow, at the north-eastern end, had its higher end pointing to the head of the South Winterborne valley. The view from a second long barrow to the east is also angled north towards this river valley, but this time the mound is oriented *along* the dry valley. To form the bank barrow the first long barrow was massively extended to the south-west, and as one walks along it, an all-round wide-ranging view which embraces the Bride valley and the sea beyond, as well as the South Winterborne valley, is gradually revealed. On Black Down, just to the south-east of Martin's Down, there are two more very long barrows. The northern one (6d on **46**) lies at a lower level on the north-facing slope and, like the original small long barrow on the top of Martin's Down, and the one immediately east of that, possesses the typical blocked south-western horizon and a commanding view down into the river valley at Poor Lot. On the other hand, the higher and larger of the two barrows on Black Down (6i on **46**) has, from its higher south-eastern end, a fine view of the Bride valley, Golden Cap and the sea. In all three cases, it could be argued that the longer bank barrows were a later development, with the more imposing monuments also commanding quite different sitings in visual terms. If this were so, then it may be that whatever rituals had been connected with the relatively hidden smaller long barrows, with their inward looking riverine visual focusing, were later overtaken by activities which were more wide-ranging in scope and incorporated a strong element of contemplation relating to the ocean. In this respect it is also interesting to note that the two shorter barrows which have strong sea views – the Grey Mare and Hell Stone — were not connected visually with the small localised groups of the valley barrows. These two monuments are also the only known to have incorporated substantial structures of stone. Perhaps they were relatively later in date and more connected, both functionally and visually, to the bank barrows.

Viewing a wider world: the Lanceborough King Barrow

As part of his arguments in favour of barrows having been used as focal points for rituals and ceremonies carried out by the living, John Barrett pointed out that some barrows may have functioned as platforms, in both the architectural and theatrical sense. Certain barrows are very large, or were gradually heightened, and these mounds often possess flat tops. In most counties there are a few such mounds, which could be called aggrandised barrows. We have mentioned before the very large single barrows associated with some of the large henge enclosures in Wessex: the Hatfield Barrow at Marden, the Great Barrow at Knowlton (*see* **49**) and Conquer Barrow at Mount Pleasant. Such aggrandised mounds are so high that it is unlikely that they have been reduced much in size over the years, so they can still be recognised and defined in terms of their superlative height.

Some aggrandised barrows, however, are defined rather by their very large diameter and elaborate structural features. Such a barrow is the massive 'bell-disc' barrow, Bincombe G60f, which lies on the South Dorset Ridgeway and can be seen towards the right edge of the aerial view in figure **73**. This monument which, with its outer bank, resembles a small henge as much as a classic round barrow, occupies a col position where the Ridgeway narrowly passes between the heads of two steep dry valleys. Many of the barrows visible in the adjacent ploughed fields were excavated by Edward Cunnington and his Ridgeway barrow 7; the one which produced the gold dagger pommel (**54**), is situated in the pale reservoir enclosure near the top right-hand corner of the air photograph. Also in south-east Dorset there are six barrows which are 14ft (4.3m) high or more. These include Conquer Barrow and Clandon (*see* **colour plate 22**), but the highest of all is the Lanceborough King Barrow (**colour plate 29**). This magnificent barrow, now isolated and covered with nettles in the middle of a ploughed field, lies just east of Maiden Castle and is closely associated with a long barrow, an enclosure which may have been a small henge, and three other round barrows, all now ploughed flat and mostly visible in **colour plate 29**. The only known finds are one burial, probably Roman in date, from the very top of the King Barrow.

This spot, occupied by the long barrow and small henge, had obviously been important since at least the early Neolithic. It lies within a natural basin. The King Barrow may have originated in Neolithic times and has probably been extended and gradually heightened over a long period of time. In examining the barrow on the ground, we soon realised that climbing the mound was a revelatory experience. The view at the base was restricted and enclosed, but from the level platform at the top one could see into the far distance in many directions. We therefore decided to test out these views using GIS data with viewsheds relating to ground level and to regular intervals up the mound. The resulting plots for the ground level and top platform were then related to the topography, and the lines of view, and nested horizons, were drawn out (**74** and **75**).

At ground level the site of the barrow lies within a very small basin with a tight local horizon (**74**) while a second inner horizon is defined by the Maiden Castle and Alington ridges. Beyond this views out are restricted to a vista south-east towards the Broadmayne bank barrow at Culliford Tree and glimpses only of far horizons on the heathlands and Chaldon Down to the east. At the highest platform level, the local restricted horizon has gone, so that the first horizon is defined by the Maiden Castle and Alington ridges and, now, the Clandon Barrow as well. Outer horizons are now visible to the west as well as to the south-east, but it is the far horizons that are totally transformed. To the west a long view up to the bank barrow at Martin's Down can now be experienced, while to the north and east there is a total view of the uplands of central Dorset from the North Dorset Ridge round to Purbeck (**75**). Looking inwards, people standing on the barrow, and the ceremonies they acted out, would have been visible from afar. No doubt these acts will have included the use of fire and smoke; certainly the upper layers of the large Clandon Barrow were composed entirely of horizontal layers of ash (*see* **21**).

Throughout early prehistory the slight spur of land at Lanceborough was a platform from which the world could be viewed, both in a physical and metaphorical sense. To begin with this world was enclosed and bounded by a series of monuments standing in profile on a close inner horizon — the long barrow to the west, the Maiden Castle bank barrow,

73 *An aggrandised barrow on the South Dorset Ridgeway: bell-disc Bincombe G60f. This large barrow is unexcavated but many of the ploughed barrows in this view were explored by Edward Cunnington. Ridgeway 7, which contained the gold pommel illustrated in figure* **54**, *is located in the reservoir enclosure near the top right-hand corner of this view.* (© Crown copyright. NMR)

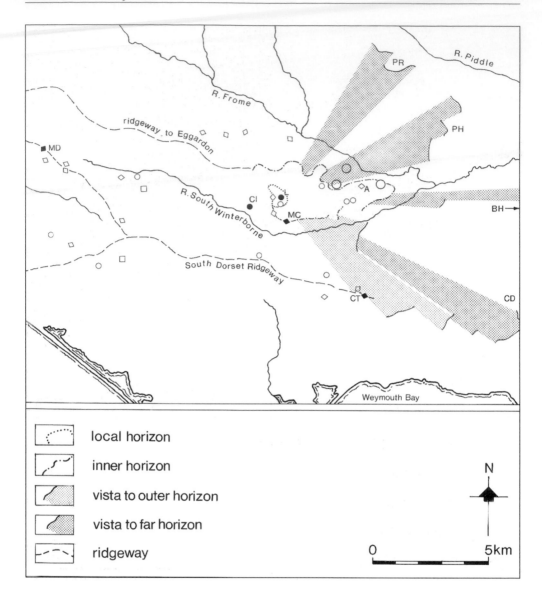

74 *Lanceborough: the view out from ground level. A Alington; BH Bovington Heath; Cl Clandon; CT Culliford Tree; L Lanceborough; MC Maiden Castle; MD Martin's Down; PH Puddletown Heath; PR Puddletown ridge; CD Chaldon Down.* (Ann and Peter Woodward)

Alington long barrow and Mount Pleasant henge. As the King Barrow platform was raised skywards, it became possible to view and integrate places on more distant horizons. Also there was now a visual link to the enlarged Clandon Barrow. And Clandon would have provided further vistas to the Ridgeway and to the north-west. Both Lanceborough and Clandon were substantial architectural statements from which certain men and women would have been able to define new boundaries and regulate a wider world.

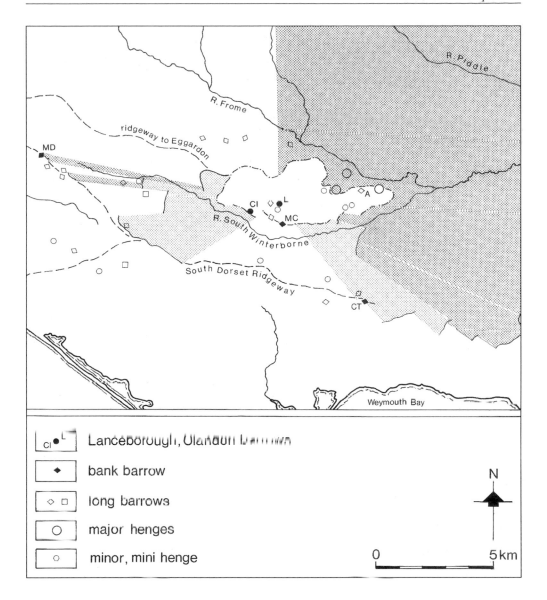

75 *Lanceborough: the view out from the top of the King Barrow. A Alington; Cl Clandon; CT Culliford Tree; L Lanceborough; MC Maiden Castle; MD Martin's Down.* (Ann and Peter Woodward)

Notes

Introductions to the theory and practice of phenomenology can be found in Tilley 1994 and Thomas 1996. The account of the Black Mountains long cairns is in Tilley 1994, chapter 4; for Andrew Fleming's rejoinder see Fleming 1999.

Tor and grounder cairns are defined in Johnson and Rose 1994, 34-42. Their symbolism and that of dolmens is considered in Tilley 1995, Tilley 1994, 87-109 and

Bradley 1998. For Parc le Broes Cym, see Whittle and Wysocki 1998, 141 and 176-7. The symbolism of dolines is discussed in Tilley 1999, 225-9; the quotation is from pages 228-9. For the Yorkshire sink holes see Manby 1974, 77 and Hayfield et al 1991, 396-9 and figure 6. The Hambledon Hill long barrows are described in Mercer 1980, 40-44; the quotation is from page 63.

The arguments concerning circles of barrows around Dorchester, Avebury and Stonehenge are presented in Woodward 1991, Woodward and Woodward 1996, and Parker Pearson and Ramilisonina 1998. Richard Bradley's book is Bradley 1998.

For a brief introductory discussion of the human senses see MacGregor 1999. Colour symbolism is discussed in Lynch 1998 and Jones 1999; acoustic effects in Watson and Keating 1999.

The publication of the Stonehenge barrows project will be Exon et al forthcoming; for Loughcrew see Fraser 1998.

The south Dorset long barrows and Lanceborough King Barrow analyses were undertaken by Peter and Ann Woodward using viewsheds generated by Sally Exon.

The long barrow intervisibility patterns presented here are not the same as those listed in Tilley 1999, table 6.1. This is mainly due to the fact that the computerised data supplies verification for view lines that are today obscured by trees. For discussion of mounds as platforms, see Barrett 1994.

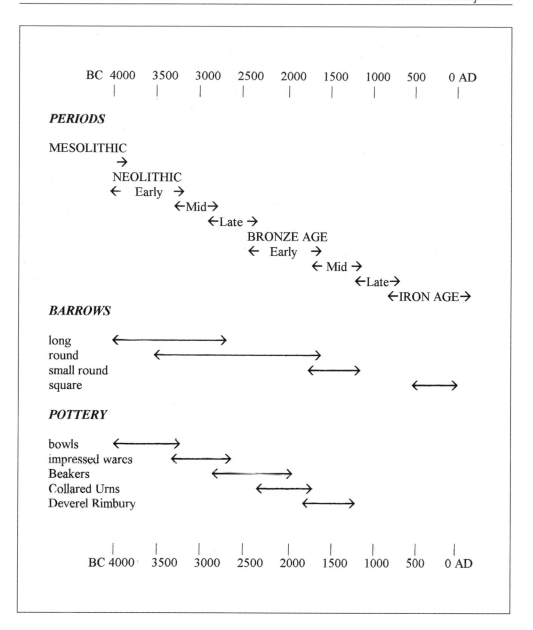

76 *A time chart for British barrows in prehistory*

References

Annable, F.K. and Simpson, D.D.A., *Guide catalogue of the Neolithic and Bronze Age collections of Devizes Museum* Devizes 1964

Ashbee, P.A., *The Bronze Age Barrow in Britain* London: Phoenix 1960

Ashbee, P., 'The Fussell's Lodge long barrow excavations, 1957', *Archaeologia* 100, 1-80. 1966

Ashbee, P., *The Earthen Long Barrow in Britain* London: Dent 1970

Ashbee, P., 'Amesbury barrow 51: excavation 1960', *Wiltshire Archaeological and Natural History Magazine* 70-71, 1-60. 1978

Ashbee, P., 'The excavation of Amesbury barrows 58, 61a, 61, 72', *Wiltshire Archaeological and Natural History Magazine* 79, 39-91. 1985

Ashbee, P., Smith, I.F. and Evans, J.G., 'Excavation of three long barrows near Avebury, Wiltshire', *Proceedings of the Prehistoric Society* 45, 207-300. 1979

Ashbee, P., Bell, M. and Proudfoot, E., *Wilsford Shaft: Excavations 1960-62* English Heritage Archaeological Report no.11, London. 1989

Atkinson, R.J.C., Brailsford, J.W. and Wakefield, H.G., 'A pond barrow at Winterbourne Steepleton, Dorset' *Archaeological Journal* 108, 1-24. 1951

Barclay, A., Gray, M. and Lambrick, G., *Excavations at the Devil's Quoits, Stanton Harcourt, Oxfordshire, 1972-3 and 1988* Oxford: Thames Valley Landscapes: the Windrush Valley 3. 1995

Barclay, A. and Halpin, C., *Excavations at Barrow Hills, Radley, Oxfordshire. Volume 1: The Neolithic and Bronze Age Monument Complex.* Oxford: Thames Valley Landscapes Volume 11. 1999

Barnatt, J., 'Taming the land: Peak District farming and ritual in the Bronze Age', *Derbyshire Archaeological Journal* 119, 19-78. 1999

Barnatt, J. and Smith, K., *The Peak District: Landscapes Through Time* London: Batsford/English Heritage 1997

Barrett, J.C., 'The living, the dead and the ancestors: Neolithic and Early Bronze Age mortuary practices' in J.C. Barrett and I.A. Kinnes (eds.), *The Archaeology of Context in the Neolithic and Bronze Age: Recent Trends* Sheffield: University of Sheffield 1988

Barrett, J.C., *Fragments from Antiquity* Oxford: Blackwell 1994

Barrett, J., Bradley, R. and Green, M., *Landscape, monuments and society. The prehistory of Cranborne Chase* Cambridge: Cambridge University Press 1991

Bender, B., Hamilton, S. and Tilley, C., 'Leskernick: Stone Worlds; Alternative Narratives; Nested Landscapes', *Proceedings of the Prehistoric Society* 63, 147-178. 1997

Bradley, R., '"Various styles of urn" — cemeteries and settlements in southern England' in R. Chapman, I. Kinnes and K. Randsborg (eds.) *The Archaeology of Death* 93-104. Cambridge: Cambridge University Press 1981

Bradley, R., *The Significance of Monuments* London: Routledge 1998

Bradley, R., 'Ruined buildings, ruined stones: enclosures, tombs and natural places in the Neolithic of south-west England' *World Archaeology* 30(1), 13-22. 1998

Brewster, T.C.M., 'Garton Slack', *Current Archaeology* No. 51, Vol. 5,4, 104-116. 1976

Brown, L., Corney, M. and Woodward, P.J., 'An Iron Age and Romano-British settlement on Oakley Down, Wimborne St Giles, Dorset', *Proceedings of the Dorset Natural History and Archaeological Society* 117, 67-79. 1995

Burgess, C., *The Age of Stonehenge* London: Dent 1980

Burl, A., *The Stone Circles of the British Isles* London: Yale University Press 1976

Burl, A., *Prehistoric Avebury* London: Yale University Press 1979

Case, H.J., 'The Lambourn Seven Barrows', *Berkshire Archaeological Journal* 55, 15-31. 1957

Case, H.J., 'The Vicarage Field, Stanton Harcourt' in H.J. Case and A.W.R. Whittle (eds.) *Settlement Patterns in the Oxford region: excavations at the Abingdon causewayed enclosure and other sites* 103-17. London: Council for British Archaeology Research Report 44. 1982

Christie, P.M., 'Crig-a-Mennis: a Bronze Age barrow at Liskey, Perranzabuloe, Cornwall', *Proceedings of the Prehistoric Society* 26, 76-97. 1960

Christie, P.M., 'A barrow cemetery of the second millennium BC in Wiltshire, England', *Proceedings of the Prehistoric Society* 33, 336-366. 1967

Clark, J.G.D., *Symbols of Excellence* Cambridge: Cambridge University Press 1985

Clarke, D.L., *Beaker Pottery of Great Britain and Ireland* Cambridge: Cambridge University Press 1970

Clarke, D.V., Cowie, T.G. and Foxon, A., *Symbols of Power at the Time of Stonehenge* Edinburgh: HMSO 1985

Cleal, R. and Allen, M., 'Investigation of tree-damaged barrows on King Barrow Ridge, Amesbury', *Wiltshire Archaeological and Natural History Magazine* 87, 54-84. 1994

Darvill, T.C., *The megalithic chambered tombs of the Cotswold-Severn region* Highworth: Vorda 1982

Dent, J., 'Cemeteries and settlement patterns of the Iron Age of the Yorkshire Wolds', *Proceedings of the Prehistoric Society* 48, 437-57. 1982

Donaldson, P., 'The excavation of a multiple round barrow at Barnack, Cambridgeshire 1974-1976', *Antiquaries Journal* 57, 197-231. 1977

Drew, C.D. and Piggott, S.P., 'The excavation of long barrow 163a on Thickthorn Down, Dorset', *Proceedings of the Prehistoric Society* 2, 77-96. 1936a

Drew, C.D. and Piggott, S.P., 'Two Bronze Age barrows excavated by Mr Edward Cunnington', *Proceedings of the Dorset and Natural History Society* 58, 18-25. 1936b

Drewett, P., Rudling, D. and Gardiner, M., *The South-East to AD 1000* London: Longman 1988

Ellison, A., 'Deverel-Rimbury urn cemeteries: the evidence for social organisation' in J.C. Barrett and R. Bradley (eds.) *Settlement and Society in the British Later Bronze Age* 115-26. Oxford: British Archaeological Reports 83. 1980

Ellison, A., 'Towards a socio-economic model for the Middle Bronze Age in southern England' in I. Hodder, G. Isaac and N. Hammond (eds.) *Pattern of the Past: studies in honour of David Clarke* 413-38. Cambridge: Cambridge University Press 1981

Exon, S., Gaffney, V., Woodward, A. and Yorston, R., *Stonehenge Landscapes* forthcoming

Field, D., 'Round barrows and the harmonious landscape; placing Early Bronze Age burial monuments in south-east England', *Oxford Journal of Archaeology* 17 No. 3, 309-326. 1998

Fleming, A., 'Territorial patterns in Bronze Age Wessex', *Proceedings of the Prehistoric Society* 37, 138-66. 1971

Fleming, A., 'Phenomenology and the megaliths of Wales: a dreaming too far?', *Oxford Journal of Archaeology* 18 no. 2, 119-126. 1999

Fox, C., *Life and Death in the Bronze Age* London: Routledge 1959

Fraser, S.M., 'The public forum and the space between: the materiality of social strategy in the Irish Neolithic', *Proceedings of the Prehistoric Society* 64, 203-24. 1999

French, C.A.I., *Excavation of the Deeping St. Nicholas barrow complex, south Lincolnshire* Lincoln: Lincolnshire Archaeological Heritage Report Series 1. 1994

Gray, H.StG. and Prideaux, C.S., 'Barrow-digging at Martinstown, near Dorchester, 1903', *Proceedings of the Dorset Natural History and Archaeological Society* 26, 6-39. 1905

Green, C. and Rollo-Smith, S., 'The excavation of eighteen round barrows near Shrewton, Wiltshire', *Proceedings of the Prehistoric Society* 50, 255-318. 1984

Green, H.S., 'Early Bronze Age territory and population in Milton Keynes, Buckinghamshire and the Great Ouse valley', *Archaeological Journal* 131, 75-139. 1973

Greenwell, W. and Rolleston, G., *British Barrows* Oxford: Clarendon Press 1877

Grinsell, L.V., *Victoria County History. A History of Wiltshire. Volume 1, part 1* Oxford: Oxford University Press 1957

Grinsell, L.V., *Dorset Barrows* Dorchester: Dorset Archaeological and Natural History Society 1959

Grinsell, L.V., 'Somerset Barrows. Part II: north and east', *Somerset Archaeological and Natural History Society* 115, 44-137. 1971

Grinsell, L.V., 'Disc-barrows', *Proceedings of the Prehistoric Society* 40, 79-112. 1974

Grinsell, L.V., *Folklore of Prehistoric Sites in Britain* Newton Abbot: David and Charles 1976

Grinsell, L.V., *Dorset Barrows Supplement* Dorchester: Dorset Archaeological and Natural History Society 1982

Grinsell, L.V., *Barrows in England and Wales* Princes Risborough: Shire 1990

Hall, D.N. and Woodward, P.J., 'Radwell excavations, 1974-75; the Bronze Age ring ditches', *Bedfordshire Archaeological Journal* 12, 1-16. 1977

Hayfield, C., Pouncett, J. and Wagner, P., 'Vessey Ponds: a "prehistoric" water supply in East Yorkshire?', *Proceedings of the Prehistoric Society* 61, 393-408. 1995

Hoare, R.C., *The Ancient History of Wiltshire. Volumes 1 and 2* London 1812 and 1821

Hughes, E.G., *The Lockington Gold Hoard: an Early Bronze Age Barrow Cemetery at Lockington, Leicestershire* Oxford: Oxbow monograph, in press

Hughes, I., 'Megaliths: space, time and the landscape. A view from the Clyde', *Scottish Archaeological Review* 5, 41-56. 1988

Johnson, N. and Rose, P., *Bodmin Moor; an Archaeological Survey, vol.1: The Human Landscape to c.1800* Truro and Cornwall: Cornwall Archaeological Unit, English Heritage (Archaeological Report no. 24) and Royal Commission on the Historical Monuments of England (Supplementary Series no. 11) 1994

Jones, A., 'Local colour: megalithic architecture and colour symbolism in Neolithic Arran', *Oxford Journal of Archaeology* 18, no. 4, 339-50. 1999

Kinnes, I., *Round Barrows and Ring-ditches in the British Neolithic* London: British Museum Occasional Papers 7, 1979

Kinnes, I., *Non-Megalithic Long Barrows and Allied Structures in the British Neolithic* London: British Museum Occasional Papers 52. 1992

Kinnes, I. and Longworth, I., *Catalogue of the Excavated Prehistoric and Romano-British material in the Greenwell Collection* London: British Museum Press 1985

Leach, J.W. and Leach, E., *The Kula: new perspectives on Massim exchange* Cambridge: Cambridge University Press 1983

Longworth, I.H., *Collared Urns of the Bronze Age in Great Britain and Ireland* Cambridge: Cambridge University Press 1984

Lynch, F., 'The contents of excavated tombs in north Wales' in T.G.E. Powell et al *Megalithic Enquiries in the West of Britain* Liverpool: Liverpool University Press 1969

Lynch, F., *Excavations in the Brenig Valley, a Mesolithic and Bronze Age Landscape in North Wales* Aberystwyth: Cambrian Archaeological Monograph 5. 1993

Lynch, F., *Megalithic Tombs and Long Barrows in Britain* Princes Risborough: Shire 1997

Lynch, F., 'Colour in prehistoric architecture' in A. Gibson and D. Simpson (eds.) *Prehistoric Ritual and Religion* 62-7. Stroud: Sutton 1998

MacGregor, G., 'Making sense of the past in the present: a sensory analysis of carved stone balls', *World Archaeology* 31(2), 258-71. 1999

Malone, C., *Avebury.* London: Batsford and English Heritage 1989

Malinowski, B., *Argonauts of the Western Pacific: An Account of Native Enterprise and Adventure in the Archipelagos of Melanesian New Guinea* London: Routledge 1922

Manby, T.G., 'The excavation of the Willerby Wold Long Barrow, East Riding of Yorkshire, England', *Proceedings of the Prehistoric Society* 29, 173-205. 1963

Manby, T., *Grooved Ware Sites in Yorkshire and the North of England* Oxford: British Archaeological Reports 9. 1974

Marsden, B.M., *The Early Barrow Diggers* Stroud: Tempus 1999

Mercer, R., *Hambledon Hill. A Neolithic Landscape* Edinburgh: Edinburgh University Press 1980

Miles, W.A., *A Description of the Deverel Barrow* London: Nichols and Son 1826

Mizoguchi, K., 'A historiography of a linear barrow cemetery: a structurationist's point of view', *Archaeological Review from Cambridge* 11, 40-9. 1993

Morgan, F. de M., 'The excavation of a long barrow at Nutbane, Hampshire', *Proceedings of the Prehistoric Society* 25, 15-51. 1959

Parker Pearson, M., 'The Earlier Bronze Age' in J. Hunter and I. Ralston (eds.) *The Archaeology of Britain* London: Routledge 1999

Parker Pearson, M., and Ramilisonina, 'Stonehenge for the ancestors: the stones pass on the message', *Antiquity* 72, 308-26. 1998

Petersen, F., 'Traditions of multiple burial in later Neolithic and Early Bronze Age England', *Archaeological Journal* 129, 22-55. 1972

Piggott, S.P., 'The Early Bronze Age in Wessex', *Proceedings of the Prehistoric Society* 4, 52-106. 1938

Piggott, S.P., 'From Salisbury Plain to South Siberia', *Wiltshire Archaeological and Natural History Magazine* 58, 93-7. 1962

Pryor, F., French, C. et al, *The Fenland Project, No. 1: Archaeology and Environment in the Lower Welland Valley, Volume 2* Cambridge: East Anglian Archaeology 27. 1985

Rahtz, P., *Little Ouseburn Barrow 1958* York: York University Archaeological Publications 7. 1989

Renfrew, C., *Before Civilisation: the Radiocarbon Revolution and Prehistoric Europe* London 1973

Roese, H.E., 'Some aspects of topographical locations of Neolithic and Bronze Age monuments in Wales. III. Round cairns and round barrows', *Bulletin of the Board of Celtic Studies* 29, part II, 575-87. 1981

RCHME, *An Inventory of Historical Monuments in the County of Dorset. Volume One* London: HMSO 1952

RCHME, *An Inventory of Historical Monuments in the County of Dorset. Volume Two. South-East.* London: HMSO 1970

RCHME, *An Inventory of Historical Monuments in the County of Dorset. Volume Five. East Dorset* London: HMSO 1975

RCHME, *Long Barrows in Hampshire and the Isle of Wight* London: HMSO 1979

RCHME, *The Archaeology of Bokerley Dyke* London: HMSO 1990

Scott, W.L., 'The chambered tomb of Pant y Saer, Anglesey', *Archaeologia Cambrensis* 88, 185-228. 1933

Sherratt, A.G., 'Sacred and profane substances: the ritual use of narcotics in later Neolithic Europe' in P. Garwood, D. Jennings, R. Skeates and J. Toms (eds.) *Sacred and Profane* Oxford: Oxford University Committee for Archaeology Monograph No. 32. 1991

Sherratt, A.G., 'Introduction: Peculiar substances' and 'Chapter 1: Alcohol and its alternatives: symbol and substance in pre-industrial cultures' in J. Goodman, P.E. Lovejoy and A. Sherratt (eds.) *Consuming Habits. Drugs in History and Anthropology* London: Routledge 1995

Smith, I.F., *Windmill Hill and Avebury: Excavations by Alexander Keiller 1925-1939* Oxford: Clarendon Press 1965

Smith, I.F. and Simpson, D.D.A., 'Excavation of a Round Barrow on Overton Hill, North Wiltshire, England', *Proceedings of the Prehistoric Society* 32, 122-155. 1966

Smith, R.W., 'The ecology of Neolithic farming systems as exemplified by the Avebury region of Wiltshire', *Proceedings of the Prehistoric Society* 50, 99-120. 1984

Spratt, D.A., *Prehistoric and Roman Archaeology of North-East Yorkshire* Oxford: British Archaeological Reports British Series 104. 1982

Stoertz, C., *Ancient Landscapes of the Yorkshire Wolds. Aerial photographic transcription and analysis* Swindon: RCHME 1997

Taylor, A.F. and Woodward, P.J., 'A Bronze Age barrow cemetery, and associated settlement at Roxton, Bedfordshire', *Archaeological Journal* 142, 73-149. 1985

Taylor, J., 'Space and place: some thoughts on Iron Age and Romano-British landscapes.' in A. Gwilt and C. Haselgrove (eds.) *Reconstructing Iron Age Societies* Oxford: Oxbow Monograph 71. 1997

Thomas, J., *Time, Culture and Identity* London: Routledge 1996

Thomas, N. and Thomas, C., 'Excavations at Snail Down, Everleigh: 1953, 1955. An interim report', *Wiltshire Natural History and Archaeological Magazine* 61, 127-148. 1956

Tilley, C., *A Phenomenology of Landscape: Places, Paths and Monuments* Oxford: Berg 1994

Tilley, C., 'Rocks as resources: landscapes and power', *Cornish Archaeology* 34, 5-57. 1995

Tilley, C., *Metaphor and Material Culture* Oxford: Blackwell 1999

Tomalin, D.J., 'Combe-cluster barrow cemeteries in the Isle of Wight', *Proceedings of the Isle of Wight Natural History and Archaeological Society* 11, 85-96. 1993

Tomalin, D.J., 'Towards a new strategy for curating the Bronze Age landscape of the Hampshire and Solent region' in D.A. Hinton and M. Hughes (eds.) *Archaeology of Hampshire: a Framework for the Future* Salisbury: Hampshire County Council 1996

Watson, A. and Keating, D., 'Architecture and sound: an acoustic analysis of megalithic monuments in prehistoric Britain', *Antiquity* 73, 325-37. 1999

Watson, M.D., 'Ring-Ditches of the Upper Severn Valley.' in M. Carver (ed.) *Prehistory in Lowland Shropshire* 9-14. Shrewsbury: Shropshire Archaeological Society 1991

White, D.A., 'The excavation of an Iron Age round barrow near Handley, Dorset, 1969', *Antiquaries Journal*, 50, 26-36. 1970

White, D.A., *The Bronze Age Cremation Cemeteries at Simons Ground, Dorset* Dorchester: Dorset Archaeological and Natural History Society Monograph 3. 1982

Whittle, A. and Wysocki, M., 'Parc le Broes Cwm transepted long cairn, Gower, West Glamorgan: date, contents, and context', *Proceedings of the Prehistoric Society* 64, 139-82. 1998

Woodward, A., 'The cult of relics in prehistoric Britain' in M. Carver (ed.) *In Search of Cult: Archaeological Investigations in Honour of Philip Rahtz* Woodbridge: Boydell Press 1993

Woodward, P.J., *The South Dorset Ridgeway. Survey and excavations 1977-84*, Dorset Natural History and Archaeological Society Monograph No. 8, Dorchester. 1991

Woodward, A. and Woodward, P., 'The topography of some barrow cemeteries in Bronze Age Wessex', *Proceedings of the Prehistoric Society* 62, 275-91. 1996

Wymer, J., 'Excavation of the Lambourn long barrow', *Berkshire Archaeological Journal* 62, 1-16. 1966

Index

County abbreviations: